# The Teacher's Survival Guide

*2nd Edition*

Angela Thody, Barbara Gray and
Derek Bowden, with Amber Lascelle
and Graham Welch

**continuum**
LONDON • NEW YORK

**Continuum**

The Tower Building                          15 East 26th Street
11 York Road                               New York
London SE1 7NX                             NY 10010

First published 2000

**British Library Cataloguing-in-Publication Data**
A catalogue record for this book is available from the British Library.

ISBN   0-8264-7516-7 (paperback)

Typeset by Kenneth Burnley, Wirral, Cheshire
Printed and bound in Great Britain by MPG Books Ltd, Bodmin, Cornwall

# Contents

The authors                                                                    vii
Preface                                                                         ix
Authors' note                                                                    x

**Part One: Beginnings**
1   Success starts here   *Angela Thody*                                          3

**Part Two: Success with Pupils**
2   Creating a positive learning environment   *Barbara Gray*                    19
3   Managing difficult situations   *Barbara Gray*                               39
4   Voice management   *Graham Welch*                                            47

**Part Three: Success with Colleagues**
5   Your professional role   *Barbara Gray*                                      65
6   Your place in your school   *Derek Bowden*                                   75
7   Significant others   *Angela Thody and Barbara Gray*                         91

**Part Four: Success with Yourself**
8   Time management   *Derek Bowden*                                            105
9   Stress management   *Angela Thody*                                          119

**Part Five: Success with Your Career**
10   Your career in schools   *Angela Thody*                                    137
11   Education careers outside schools   *Angela Thody*                         153
12   Supply teaching and examining   *Amber Lascelle*                           163

**Part Six: Endings?**
13   Epilogue   *Angela Thody*                                                  181

Bibliography                                                                    183
Useful addresses                                                               186
Index                                                                          197

*To our families and friends for their support*

*and to the hundreds of colleagues*

*and thousands of children*

*who made teaching a good life.*

# The authors

**Angela Thody is** Emerita Professor of Educational Leadership at the International Institute of Educational Leadership (IIEL), University of Lincoln. Her teaching career began with the 16+ age group and then extended into higher education at the universities of Leicester, Luton, De Montfort, Open and Lincoln. While taking a career break for family development, she freelanced in playgroups, primary and secondary schools and adult education. She directed and lectured on doctoral programmes at the IIEL and has researched and published extensively including six books (one on teachers' careers), 50 articles and numerous conference presentations. She has run short courses for teachers seeking career advancement and has lectured worldwide on teaching issues. She was the first female President of the Commonwealth Council for Educational Administration and Management. She has been governor of two secondary schools and an infants school.

**Barbara Gray** is a Lincolnshire primary school headteacher. Her career began with eleven years in primary schools as a teacher before moving to her first headship. She then became a lecturer in a higher education college, teaching initial teacher training courses, taking primary school inspections, leading school professional development courses and offering consultancy. She followed this with a Senior Lectureship in Educational Leadership and Directorship of Primary School Leadership and Development Programmes at the University of Lincolnshire and Humberside until returning to primary school headships.

**Derek Bowden** was Principal of a Cheshire comprehensive secondary school and consultant to local education authorities on leadership development, appraisal and school effectiveness. His teaching experience includes work in Nigerian and British secondary schools, a sixth-form college and a further education college. He spent a period of time seconded to industry researching management training. He has lectured at the universities of Hull, Leicester, Lincolnshire and Humberside, Manchester Metropolitan and for the Open University. He has been a governor of an FE college and a primary school.

## Contributors

**Amber Lascelle** followed graduation from Cambridge and a Post Graduate Certificate in Education, with teaching English in a secondary comprehensive school. Seeking time and money to travel abroad and to retrain as a textile artist, she moved to supply teaching and has gained experience in special, secondary and primary schools in six Local Education Authorities (LEAs) in England. She also works as a marker, having been employed by five different examination organizations covering Key Stage III, GCSE and AS/A level equivalents. Her e-book on supply teaching was published in 2003 (*Supply on Demand* – Excelearnt).

**Graham Welch** is Professor and Director of Educational Research and Pro-Dean at the University of Surrey, Roehampton, following six years as Dean of the Faculty of Education. He is also Director of the Centre for Advanced Studies in Music Education (ASME), which he founded in 1990 and which has attracted over £30,000 in research funding. Graham is co-chair of the International Society for Music Education's Research Commission and chair of the Society for Research in the Psychology of Music and Music Education. His research and associated writing cover many different aspects of music and voice education. Recent media appearances have included the BBC's Cardiff 'Singer of the World' and reports of his research in *Time* magazine.

# Preface

This book is for you if you are

- in the early stages of your career in teaching;
- ready to launch to the next stage of your teaching career;
- being mentored or are mentoring student teachers or recently qualified teachers;
- responsible for staff development or appraisal for other teachers; or
- guiding recently qualified teachers in your curriculum area or department.

It's a sourcebook of ideas for education professionals to help you with developing

- your tactics in response to the initial 'fire-fighting' needs that all new teachers face;
- your later career growth; and
- your personal approaches to teaching and learning, to your colleagues and to yourself.

# Authors' note

Throughout the text the terms 'Head' or 'Headteacher' have been used to describe the school principal, as these are the most commonly used terms in England and Wales.

*Part One*

# Beginnings

# 1 Success starts here

*Angela Thody*

From the moment you enter your school's or college's site each morning – you're teaching. Even if you stand still, you're a role model transmitting subconscious, indirect and informal 'lessons'. The successful teacher needs to develop the skills to manage these 'lessons', inside and outside the classroom, so you're in control of the messages you want to send. This is what this book is about.

Your starting point is those you are managing and leading:

- your pupils (throughout this book, we use the term 'pupils' to relate to all those you may be teaching, whether classified as 'early years to 18', 'Years 1–13' or 'K through 12');
- your colleagues (senior managers, teaching and support staff);
- the significant 'others' from outside the school (parents, community members, governors, trustees, board members).

All these have expectations of you, to which you need to respond. You also have expectations of yourself to which you will want to match up.

## First impressions

What sort of teacher do you want to be? Your pupils have remarkably consistent views on this, whether they are 5, 15, 25 or 85, though how they express their conceptions may differ across the age groups.

These are some pupils' responses to the question, 'What is a good teacher?' How many of these would you have expected?

- 'We like teachers who smell nice' (secondary).
- 'We're going to be professionals, so the lecturers should look professional too' (tertiary).

- 'The first week, you should wear the same clothes each day so the children remember who you are and feel secure' (early years teacher).
- 'They should look like teachers – a bit smart' (primary).
- 'You know he's a bit different – wears a scarf every day even indoors' (tertiary).
- 'We like teachers who bother – wear something different – we can't stand XXX in that old brown thing all the time' (middle school).
- 'The ones who try to look like us, you know – the latest gear – you think, "They're not teachers yet"' (secondary).
- 'You like to feel they're approachable so they must dress rather as we do but there has to be something that sets them apart – something that indicates they know a bit more than we do' (adult education).
- 'They sort of look like they know what to do' (primary).
- 'She's got a new hair colour – it looks great' (secondary).

[For readers from outside the United Kingdom: early years = 3–5/6/7; primary = 5–11; middle = 8/9/10–11/12/13; secondary = 11–16/18; tertiary = post-16.]

You may be surprised that these views all concern teachers' visual images. We have not selected as a priority any views on how well teachers teach or know their subject or maintain discipline (though we will deal with them later, of course). We have put these views first because the visual image is what the pupils first encounter.

From the impression you make as you enter your classroom or walk the corridors, pupils form views of you that will affect the way in which they react to you.

> It's as if for generations, we have been born into . . . images which shape our expectations of what 'teacher' really means . . . It may be fruitful to work with . . . the pervasiveness and power of these images. (Weber and Mitchell, 1996, p. 123)

Hence, looking confident, looking the part and looking as if you care about what you do and how you do it are the basic essentials which reinforce good teaching and effective class leadership.

## What do pupils expect of you?

Pupils quickly see beyond the initial, visual impression they have of you. What they then expect of you is, again, consistent across age ranges. Some of the expectations pupils have of good teachers are:

- enthusiasm
- preparation
- humour
- fairness
- treating pupils as individuals
- getting marking returned quickly

*Enthusiastic* teachers are 'those who can tell us a bit more when we ask questions', who 'bother to take in pictures and make things to show us how it works' (primary). They 'add something that's not directly related to the topic but enlivens it' (tertiary). 'They just seem to like the subject – and us' (secondary).

It is easier to convey enthusiasm when you are confident that you have done a reasonable amount of lesson **preparation**. The key word is 'reasonable'. New teachers can feel somewhat daunted at trying to gain all the erudition they need as soon as they start teaching and tend to assume they need to know everything about a subject in order to teach it. The result can be over-preparation. The over-prepared teacher is usually recognized by the number of boxes of materials or piles of duplicated pages brought to the classroom, by lessons full of didactically presented information without intervening activities, and by extremely rapid delivery. Most new teachers are likely to exhibit such characteristics.

The keys to success for the over-prepared teacher are

- your willingness to find ways to summarize what you have to cover; and
- your selection of main points for in-depth coverage while relegating peripherals.

The good news is that you then find you have prepared enough material for most of the rest of the term's lessons and have spare activities for the occasional 'filler' you need when you finish a lesson more quickly than anticipated.

Over-preparation is definitely preferable to being an under-prepared teacher. How will pupils know if you are under-prepared? The same way you did when *you* were a pupil. Do you remember those teachers who

- didn't dare leave the sanctity of the front desk or whiteboard;
- had no books or papers with them;
- were easily distracted by 'red herrings' and weren't able to get the class back on track after diversionary tactics;
- filled in lessons with a great deal of colouring activities;
- arrived at the classroom later than you did and couldn't readily extract their teaching notes from an untidy pile in a tired-looking polythene carrier bag?

Those were likely to be the under-prepared teachers.

The comforting information for teachers is that pupils won't realize how much of the content of a subject you don't know, but they will know if you haven't at least tried to prepare some information or thought about how you will put over the lesson.

There will be times when you can't prepare as much as you would wish to and that's when you need the next most often quoted attribute of the effective teacher – a **sense of humour**. This is the ability to laugh at yourself, at the situation or the subject, but not to laugh at the pupils or to be sarcastic about them.

Humour is one of the few aspects of teaching that pupils do not want to be targeted individually. Otherwise, **individualized treatment** is seen as vital. Pupils respond positively to the fact that you know who they are. This is fundamental to good classroom leadership. Watch pupils' body language when you call them by name, when you give individualized praise or when you remember some personal issue on which to comment. You will see that, whatever their age, their self-esteem flourishes.

Pupils want **equal and fair** treatment with the rest of the class whatever a pupil's size, ability, assertiveness, gender, culture or other attributes. **Fairness** is interpreted by pupils as sticking to the rules. Here's an example of a situation where you need to apply fairness: *You asked for work in by a particular date and only a few have handed it in. Which of these options would you adopt (you can select more than one)?*

1. Set a new deadline for those who have not handed it in.
2. Ask those who have completed it to retain it and hand it in on the new date.
3. Congratulate those who have completed the work:
   - mark it in class with the pupils who handed it in on time (primary);
   - return it marked, for the next lesson with that class (secondary); take time at that lesson for a quiet discussion of the work with those who completed it while setting other work for the remainder to complete.
4. Moan to the whole class about their failure to hand in the work on time.
5. Delay marking work handed in late.
6. Tell the class you will accept the late work any time they can hand it in.
7. Ask each pupil whose work is not in, why this has happened and keep a list of the names and reasons.

It's not easy to select an option that will work every time, but too many teachers go for options 1 or 6. Is that fair to those who did get it in on time? What will happen next time you set a deadline?

Finally, what about your deadlines? The sooner you can **return marked work** the better, but when you are on your sixth consecutive 'working 'til midnight' day in a week, even your spirit may weaken. Accept that you have to relax sometimes and that no one is perfect.

All these points apply whatever the subject, or age group, you are teaching. A new entrant to the profession summed it up as:

We're now teachers first and subject specialists second . . . If you're a teacher you should be able to teach just about anything . . . I'll have . . . to think myself into sharing the position of the same 'non-understanding' that my pupils are likely to have . . . This is where tactics rather than subject knowledge will have to come in. (New secondary school English teacher, interview, 1999)

**Part Two** of this book (**Success with Pupils**) will help you to develop your skills with pupils. The addresses list at the back of this book lists associations which can assist you with further advice.

---

### STARTING POINTS TIP 1 – PUPILS

Learn pupils' names in the following ways:

- Learn the register list by heart, then call out names and look vaguely in the direction of the whole class – the owner of the name will respond (usually!).
- Ask one pupil to give his/her name, ask the next pupil to repeat the first name and to add his/her own name, ask the third pupil to repeat the first and second name and then to add his/her own and so on around the whole class; you will be the last one to speak, repeating all the names in order and adding your own. (It really is much easier than it sounds and is most effective; the repetition of the names aids learning and the occasional forgetfulness in repetition gives rise to good humour.)
- If names prove difficult to remember, use real, or pretend, characteristics to personalize your pupil responses, e.g. 'Now let's hear from the boy with the fantastic voice . . . the girl who always concentrates so well', etc. You can then point at anyone, but the pupils feel you know them.
- *Always* make eye contact.

---

## What do your colleagues expect of you?

Satisfying pupils' needs is the first part of being a successful teacher, but it is not the whole of it. You have to keep your colleagues happy as well as your pupils.

You may recollect the film, *Dead Poets' Society* (David Weir, Director, 1989) or the book, *The Prime of Miss Jean Brodie* (Muriel Spark, 1961), in which the heroes were eventually dismissed for being unconventional teachers who entranced their pupils but annoyed their colleagues. These are common myths, especially in times when a stereotyped view of what it means to be a teacher has emerged from competency listings, appraisal mechanisms, efforts to institute performance-related pay and teacher ratings by inspectors from government agencies (such as OFSTED, the Office for Standards in

Education in England and Wales, or the ERO, Education Review Office in New Zealand).

Before attempting to become a standardized clone to meet these demands, reflect on successful teachers you have encountered in your current or past schools or colleges. You will realize from these examples that there is scope for personality and individuality. These are vital to the success of your teaching, but you'll notice that teachers also need to fit into what is organizationally acceptable. Fitting in with the organization of a school or college includes

- being willing to participate in matters other than those which are directly subject or class related (you could be part of the team running the school disco or representing the newly qualified teachers' views on the working group considering wider option choices for the 16–18 age group);
- keeping your pupils' records up-to-date so your curriculum co-ordinator or head of department can easily access them;
- joining in school social events;
- facing a decision of whether or not to strike or work to rule or to demonstrate support for striking colleagues in other ways;
- making sure that you've given out the right forms to pupils going on a school visit so that the administrator and office staff can complete the organization of the visit on time;
- checking that the pupils have tidied up the room before leaving, or that the windows are closed, so the site staff can be confident that the facilities are ready for the community classes in the evening and that the school meets its energy-saving targets;
- bringing youthful zest and support to a more tired, older staff.

These are all positive examples, but what about negative situations when you have to say 'No' to requests? You're busy – someone else is busy; you are in the early years of your career so it's to you that tasks such as those listed above can be delegated.

---

**SCENARIO**

School corridor, end of school day. You are returning to the staffroom laden with marking and you have a meeting to attend. In passing, the headteacher cheerfully stops you for a chat including, 'We're looking for someone to start a newcomers' choir – heard you're a singer – would you be willing to give it a go?' Can you refuse? How do you refuse?

---

And it's not just refusing the headteacher that can be problematic. A primary schoolteacher recounted his first day:

> As I crossed the playground, laden with all the bags and baggage of the first-time appointee, the caretaker chatted to me, asking if I wanted the children to use sand – the caretaker intimated that sand was not welcome so I agreed that I did not use sand. 'What about water play?' was his next question. I agreed that it made rather a mess and that I wouldn't use it. By the time I had reached the school door, I had relinquished paint, glue, glitter, yoghurt pots and would have lost the play bricks too if I hadn't been rescued by the school secretary.

To help you say 'No', try the following:

1. Delay the decision – request time to think about it.
2. Offer some support but opt out of leading an activity.
3. State that you would love to help but you already have agreed to help elsewhere (and be precise about what else you are doing).
4. Propose an alternative you think you could handle.

All this is part of managing to create successful relations with teachers, support staff and your senior staff. This is as much part of your joining the organization of a school or college as your relations with pupils; and the starting points for successful relations with colleagues are similar to those for successful relations with pupils. Chapters 5 and 6 of **Part Three** of this book (**Success with Colleagues**) give guidance on how you can enhance your skills in working well with the other staff in your school who are directly concerned with providing teaching.

---

**STARTING POINTS TIP 2 – COLLEAGUES**

- Learn colleagues' names and what they do.
- Ask colleagues about their jobs and share their problems before mentioning your own.
- Join willingly in most things but *not* in all; give reasons when you can't participate and/or at least indicate regret and readiness to co-operate next time.

---

## What about those significant others?

Teachers also need to relate well to the significant others concerned with pupils' learning: parents, governors and support staff. Spot the errors in the scenario in the panel below.

---

**SCENARIO**

It's Open Evening for parents to come and discuss their child's progress with the teachers.

Teacher sits behind an adult-size desk, with child-size chairs for two parents on the opposite side. Open in front of the teacher, and facing the teacher, is a set of class marks, showing each pupil's achievements in various tests and a small collection of important-looking documents. The parents have been waiting twenty minutes as previous appointments have over-run; there is a queue of other parents behind them, close enough to hear what is being said at the desk. The parents hold their daughter's report. The teacher taps the list with a pen, shaking his head and reporting to the parents, 'An average result, tries hard, nice girl, behaves well, no problems really.'

Parents: 'We'd like to help her at home more, what can we do to encourage even better work?'

Teacher: 'No need, she'll be all right. I'm sorry, we're over-running tonight and I need to see the next appointment.'

As the teacher leaves the school late that evening, he passes the caretaker waiting to lock up the school. He does not acknowledge her.

---

This scene was produced from numerous parents' complaints encountered by the authors. Of course, *you* would never make any of the mistakes in the above scenario, but some teachers do. Learning to cope with the 'significant others' of schools is as important as learning to cope with pupils and colleagues.

Satisfying pupils and colleagues is not enough. What is done in the school must now also satisfy parents and carers, outsiders elected or appointed to be involved in the governance of schools (school governors in England and Wales, school councils, committees or boards of trustees elsewhere), local education authorities (or equivalents, such as School Boards in the USA), central or states' governments and their inspectors, the local community, religious authorities where appropriate, national teachers' professional associations, and local and national employers.

Lest you should be feeling somewhat overwhelmed at meeting the demands of this disparate and extensive group, here is the good news:

- The group is so amorphous, there is not just one common opinion, but many. You, therefore, have to select the voice to which you will listen the most – and that's where your professional abilities retain their value. The choice is yours.
- The group are the voices of the outside world for which you are preparing your pupils, so those significant others have expertise of value to you.
- Some provide free, classroom or school/college labour. Parents can bind books, provide additional library opening hours, bake cakes, listen to reading, help supervise school trips, make costumes for school plays, provide the money for orchestral instruments, print the prospectus, etc.
- The governors are the strongest school supporters' clubs you could hope to find.
- If you foster good relations with the support staff, you are more likely to get help when you need it.

---

**STARTING POINTS TIP 3 –
THE SIGNIFICANT OTHERS: PARENTS,
GOVERNORS, SUPPORT STAFF**

Make the outsiders feel like insiders – learn their names, offer them as many activities as possible in which to become involved, be extremely grateful, ask their opinions profusely.

---

To develop your ideas on working with significant others, see **Chapter 7** of **Part Three (Success with Colleagues)**.

## What do you expect of yourself?

Too much, if you are anything like most other teachers. In what seem to us to be the long-ago days when we began teaching, we don't recollect the inclusion of time and stress management in our lexicon, but they now loom large for both experienced and new teachers. We do recollect working very hard, as one would expect in the early years in any profession but we don't think it averaged 52 hours per week in term time. This was a teacher's estimated work hours in England in 2002.

These long hours gave rise to political concerns and strong pressure from the teachers' associations for changes in practice. It was felt that teachers on their usual 50–60-hour weeks might be too tired to manage their classes safely, too weary to check the accuracy of the results they entered for their pupils, too exhausted to provide that sparky enthusiasm that makes for extra-quality teaching, too overworked to remember to thank the classroom assistants and photocopying technicians for their work and too worn out to enjoy personal hobbies and family life.

As a result, a national agreement was signed in 2003 to limit teachers' responsibilities and tasks and to guarantee time during the normal working day for Planning, Preparation and Assessment jobs (PPA time). This should make your time and stress management easier but at the time of writing (2004), it is too early to be sure. A National Union of Teachers survey at the beginning of 2004 found that almost half of teachers claimed not to have benefited from the changes and fewer than one in six teachers reported any workload reduction. Twice as many reported a heavier workload than reported a lighter workload since the changes. So there is some way to go before you can relax.

Once you move out of the entry-grade teaching level, you will start to take on some managerial responsibilities. We would like to ignore the fact that the competency lists of what teachers have to do is virtually the same as that for managers in commerce at the same level, but for teachers, that list has to be achieved on top of teaching; while for their colleagues in business, it is the whole of their workload. The managerial activities for which all teachers have some responsibilities in United Kingdom and Australasian schools have to be done in the time before and after classes. In other European countries and in North America, managerial responsibilities are carried out by administrators only so that teachers are less burdened but all over the world, all teachers face ever increasing demands from their governments to work harder to raise pupils' achievements. This is why you will find chapters on time and stress management in **Part Four** of this book (**Success with Yourself**) and addresses of helpful organisations at the end of this book if you need further guidance.

## What do you want for your career?

In the early years of launching yourself into a teaching career, you need to put in more hours than those for which you are paid, as you do in any profession. It will get easier as you gain more experience. As this grows, you will be considering how to advance your career, whether this remains in school/college teaching or in alternative, but related, education areas. All these options are discussed in **Part Five** (**Success with Your Career**) and the address list at the end of the book provides contact details so you can follow up your particular interests. Meanwhile, recent developments are offering new career opportunities, as the following list from England shows (other countries mirror these or have alternatives):

- extra pay for teachers who meet particular merit requirements relating to improved pupil achievements;
- increasing numbers of support staff to relieve the administrative loads of teachers (O'Sullivan *et al.,* 2000) and

government regulations on their taking over more duties previously done by teachers such as classroom displays and photocopying (2003 onwards);

- sophisticated information and communications technology to professionalize the resources used for teaching (e.g. subsidized purchase schemes for teachers' laptop computers; from 2005, England's government Department for Education and Skills launches a cable TV channel for teachers);
- career entry profiles, mentors and professional development tutors help guide new teachers;
- a National College for School Leadership and a national hierarchy of qualifications for progression through the grades of management responsibilities to headship;
- fast track entry and career development for some teachers;
- a National Curriculum saves you the time of devising your own syllabuses and, to some extent, your own teaching methods. (Not every teacher will regard this positively. See, for example, contrasting research views in, e.g. Helsby and McCulloch, 1996, and Galton *et al.*, 1999, or just start a discussion in your own staffroom!) ;
- new routes to career advancement in teaching, such as Advanced Skills Teaching;
- delegation to schools of control over their budgets means that teachers can more easily participate in decisions over who gets what resources in a school, senior managers can give much quicker responses to requests, and there is likely to be increasing scope to negotiate salaries;
- increasing numbers of options for those who want careers related to education but not in school teaching.

## The end of your beginning . . .

In the staffrooms of your schools and colleges you will meet teachers disgruntled with the job they are doing but you will also meet many who remind us of the joys of teaching:

> I still get a buzz when a pupil suddenly understands something with which he's been having difficulties and I know it was I who explained it to him.

It's a job that makes you a project manager from day one – and it relies on your own initiative to reach the project goal your way.

It's a great feeling in town on Saturday to get a cheery 'Hello' from the kid who gave you hassle on Friday.

Ask these positive teachers how they cope with the workload and the stress, and follow their examples. Read this book for more ideas and remember to 'smile, you're on stage now'.

---

### STARTING POINTS TIP 4

Start collecting a mental, or actual, file of 'things to do/talk about' when you have some unexpected time to fill before the end of a lesson.

Don't stop 'teaching' when you leave the classroom; smile and greet pupils, colleagues and visitors as you walk around your school or college.

---

*Part Two*

# Success with Pupils

# 2 Creating a positive learning environment

*Barbara Gray*

This chapter will look at a framework for promoting effective class-room management and quality learning. The framework is used to provide answers for the following questions:

- How do we create a positive context for learning?
- How do we maximize the chances of appropriate behaviour and handle the consequences of inappropriate behaviour constructively?
- How do we organize the classroom environment in order to promote appropriate behaviour and attitudes to learning?

## A framework for the development of positive behaviour

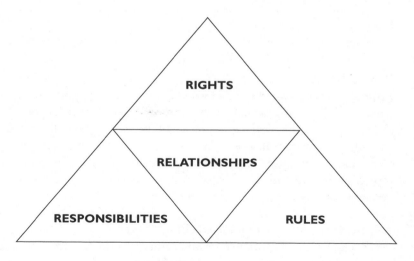

Figure 2.1

The elements of this framework work together to create a caring community of learners in which all the strands are interdependent and all are dependent on the quality of the relationships in the school.

### Rights
Everyone in the class community, including the teacher, has the right to feel safe (physically and emotionally), to be treated with dignity and respect, to be listened to, and to learn. Use Figure 2.2 to consider how your pupil, your class assistant and you would experience this in your classroom. For example, how do you ensure that everyone is listened to? For the pupil it could be that you are available at the start of the day; for the support person it could be that you make time at the end of the session; for you it could be that you have planned meetings with your mentor.

|                                   | *Pupil* | *Class assistant* | *Teacher* |
| --------------------------------- | ------- | ----------------- | --------- |
| To feel safe                      |         |                   |           |
| To be treated with dignity and respect |    |                   |           |
| To be listened to                 |         |                   |           |
| To learn                          |         |                   |           |

**Figure 2.2**

### Responsibilities
Responsibilities go hand in hand with rights; for every right there is a responsibility, since we are each accountable for our behaviour. Covey expresses this well as 'response-ability', which he defines as 'the ability to choose our response' (1989, p. 71). Does the management and organization of your class enable pupils to respond appropriately and with confidence? Are they encouraged to choose the right response? Are pupils encouraged to

- treat each other with understanding;
- look after the classroom, each other and each other's property;
- enter and leave the room appropriately and to move about the school well;

- listen to each other and express their views without risk of ridicule;
- take risks with their learning, seeing mistakes as an opportunity for learning?

If pupils are constantly ordered about and controlled, they will never learn to be self-effective. To demonstrate responsibility pupils should be given opportunities to practise. We all need to understand that we each choose our behaviour. Behaviour is the result of our own decisions, and pupils need to learn the skill of making decisions and reflecting on the effects of their choices.

---

### POSITIVE LEARNING ENVIRONMENT TIP 1

- A pupil who is told the learning objectives of a visit to the school wildlife area, and the nature of the visit, should be able to organize the resources they need and decide what extra clothing they need to bring. They will learn how to make appropriate decisions and how to be responsible.
- A pupil who is told what to take and what to wear will learn to respond to commands.

---

*What opportunities for pupil decision-making are offered in your school?*

| | |
|---|---|
| Can they choose where they sit in the hall for the daily act of worship? | |
| Can they choose who they sit next to in class? | |
| Can they express their views through a school meeting? | |
| Are they encouraged to express how they feel about certain events? | |
| When acting in an inappropriate way, are they encouraged to understand that they chose to behave in that way and that there are other choices they could make instead? | |
| Are the pupils able to choose what resources they use; for example, what size, shape, texture and colour of paper to use in art, or which equipment to use in science? | |

Figure 2.3

The pupils need skills to be able to choose to behave in certain ways. As teachers we need to develop each pupil's ability to

- have positive self-awareness, self-confidence and self-esteem;
- understand the links between their feelings and their actions;
- have ways to express their feelings;
- understand that there are choices;
- develop effective communication skills;
- develop decision-making skills.

### Rules

Rules are based on rights and responsibilities. They should form a contract between all class members, be negotiated with all in the class and be expressed in positive phrases, written in terms of what you and your pupils will do.

---

**PRACTICAL REFLECTION:
CIRCLE TIME IN ACTION**

The teacher greets her new class by telling them she has heard wonderful things about them from their last teacher. She continues by saying that she is really looking forward to working with them over the year. She challenges pupils by telling them that one of the first tasks they have to do together is to consider how they all want each other to behave.

The pupils respond positively and suggest that the class share a circle time so that they can all listen to what everyone is thinking. Agreeing, another pupil suggests that they could also discuss ideas about what their rules should be. A third pupil says they could then agree what the class rules are going to be.

- What does this approach say about the teacher's expectations?
- What does it say about the teacher's attitudes to the pupils as people?
- What does it say about the pupils' responses?
- What does it say about the school's approach to personal and social education?

---

Using Mosley's (1996) circle time approach is an excellent way to create a negotiated, shared and fair contract of behaviour which involves all the class community and creates a sense of ownership of behaviour expectations. Circle work is a way of organizing a group or class where the aims are interpersonal awareness and the development of communication skills. The whole class sits in a circle and shares perceptions, experiences, ideas or feelings. It is an excellent way for pupils to be encouraged to listen actively and for all members of the group to be heard. Even the shyest member will usually feel able to take part.

The whole-class discussion should lead to a simple statement, or contract, which all members of the class could sign. These could be displayed prominently so that visitors to the room know what the class members expect and to serve as a reminder of the agreement. For example:

---

**CLASS 8's SEPTEMBER AGREEMENT**

We all agree

- to treat others as they want to be treated;
- to be careful with other people's things;
- to make sure we help other people to learn;
- to listen to other people's ideas.

---

The behaviour contract should be changed as necessary, for example, reviewed each term, and used as the basis for PSE work. Avoid 'Don't be' rules; phrase the rules positively so emphasizing what the pupils should be doing rather than telling them what they should not be doing. Limit the number of rules to around five to help you to keep them prominent, and refer to them often. The rules should be kept alive. How will you display them? Do they need to be in picture form for some pupils?

### Relationships

Establishing effective relationships should be our top priority. Learning is enhanced or hindered by the social processes at work. When good relationships are established, we can create opportunities for personal development. If the pupils experience a climate of acceptance, their self-concept will be strengthened and interpersonal skills may be developed; positive relationships are built when individuals feel valued and respected. We should therefore develop each individual's self-esteem and interpersonal effectiveness to create the best climate for learning.

This isn't always easy, since the context of each lesson is unique, and the demands made in that lesson of each pupil, together with the support they receive, are unique; the pupils and you, their teacher, are all unique individuals. Each pupil brings many particular experiences to a situation and these will affect what you are trying to establish.

When members of the class community know and trust each other, are able to skilfully communicate with each other and are able to solve relationship problems, then you have the necessary building-blocks for creating a positive climate for learning. Genuine openness requires self-awareness and self-acceptance: you need to be able to trust, to be able to express how you feel. All members of the class community should be enabled to listen to each other and to learn how other people want to be treated.

Communication skills involve sending messages which can be understood, and listening to ensure understanding. Pupils – even very young pupils – should be able to respond in helpful ways to each other's problems.

Pupils need to be able to manage their feelings constructively. They need to learn the skills of negotiating mutually beneficial solutions. If the teacher always intercedes and acts as judge and jury, the pupils will never learn to resolve their conflicts constructively.

---

### REFLECTION

- How does your classroom measure up to this ideal?
- Which area is your priority for development, with the pupils you are teaching?

## Creating a positive context for learning

Learning takes place in a social context and we need to take account of the social processes if we are to understand and enhance the management of classroom learning.

> **POSITIVE LEARNING ENVIRONMENT TIP 2**
>
> Remember:
>
> - Changing the behaviour of a pupil effectively takes time.
>
> The change is more likely to occur if you
>
> - are clear about which behaviours need to be changed;
> - teach the behaviour you wish to see instead.

Over the last ten years there has been an increasing emphasis on a thorough knowledge of subject matter – the 'knowing what'. Teacher education has concentrated on 'knowing what' and experiences of the practical classroom, the 'knowing how'. But knowing the 'why' of pupils' learning and behaviour is vital, and we can learn a lot from the field of psychology. It is important to reflect on our practice with the insight of the underlying principles. We cannot have effective teaching and learning without the consideration of theory and our subsequent reflection on our own practice.

### *How does knowing 'why?' help us?*

Vygotsky (1978) emphasized the need to work with each pupil's 'tomorrow', where learning is a challenge, but an achievable challenge. He identified 'the zone of proximal development', the area of learning where the pupil can achieve with help and without help. 'Scaffolding', which emphasizes the supportive role the adult plays in a pupil's learning, is just as important when pupils are learning about behaviour as it is when they are learning physical or cognitive skills. We need to give the pupil support and teaching as they learn about behaviour.

McPhillimy (1996) helpfully discusses the compatibility of different psychological approaches, emphasizing the behaviourist and cognitive approaches. The behaviourists suggest the following:

- *We should deal with observable behaviour.*
  What pupils do and say are important, but their thoughts and feelings are not.
- *Behaviour is learned.*
  Behaviour is the product of our experiences, so it is possible for someone to stop behaving in one way and to start to behave in another way as a result of experiences. Learners need feedback to be able to adjust their behaviour to draw nearer to the set target.
- *Changes are governed by the consequences of our actions.*
  We need to enable trial and error learning.
- *What the teacher says and does is important.*
  The events leading to the behaviour, the setting for the event and the consequences of that action are also important.

For the behaviourists, the teacher's task is to know what is needed, to increase the desired behaviour and decrease undesired behaviour.
  Alternatively the cognitive approach stresses the following:

- *Thoughts and feelings are important, since they are the essence of the person.*
- *Seeing the classroom from the pupil's point of view is vital.*
- *Misbehaviour is seen as a symptom of the problem, rather than the problem itself.*
  A pupil who is assessed as 'not trying' may just be attempting to avoid failure.
- *An essential aspect of behaviour management is that the teacher improves a pupil's self-concept as a person and as a learner.*

Which approach drives your philosophy and style as a teacher?
  McPhillimy (1996) suggests that the important concepts from each approach can be brought together through a 'Behavioural, Reflective, Relationship approach' (BRR). In this approach you would focus on the actual behaviour, reflect on the pupil's thoughts, feelings and motives, and work with the pupils through positive relationships.

### What must a teacher do?
- Accept you have a responsibility towards each pupil's behaviour.

- Believe that misbehaviour should be stopped.
- Accept that a pupil's purposes, motives and feelings are important.
- See things from the child's point of view.
- Create warm, positive, genuine relationships.
- Understand that a pupil's self-concept has an influence on behaviour.

---

### REFLECTION

Imagine the scene: the teacher is cross about something, really telling the class off for some misdemeanour, when she spots a pupil at the back of the room mouthing what she is going to say next . . . and he is right! What does the teacher do?

- Get angry and tell the pupil off while in full flow?
- Laugh?
- Ignore?

What would the consequences of each action be?

---

Your response and the consequences of that response depend on the relationships you have developed with the class. The 'ABC' approach enables you to reflect on your behaviour as much as reflecting on the pupil's.

---

### POSITIVE LEARNING ENVIRONMENT TIP 3

Use an 'ABC' approach to understanding behaviour:

A: *Antecedent.* Look at what leads up to the situation, the setting for the behaviour.
B: *Behaviour.* Examine the actual behaviour itself.
C: *Consequences.* Look at the outcomes of the behaviour.

*What sort of teacher is likely to have pupils who behave appropriately?*

In the short term, you should

- enjoy being with pupils;
- be open and honest. Do you, for example, apologize to the pupils if you have reacted unfairly?
- collect and collate information.

In the medium term, you should

- be positive about yourself, in order to develop a social presence;
- be calm and relaxed;
- regularly find and acknowledge something good in each pupil;
- have the strategies for maintaining your own well-being so you are able to withstand frustration.

In the long term, you should

- be confident in understanding the problem and responding appropriately to the problem;
- focus on what the pupil needs to learn and what might be changed to enhance that learning;
- be able to make good judgements in evaluating others and yourself. Do you expect certain pupils to misbehave?
- seek new solutions for problems;
- reflect on your own practice.

Self-evaluation is rarely continued in any formal way after initial teacher education, and probably not picked up until higher degree work when you may be introduced to professional journals. Self-evaluation is vital for learning. Think about what you do which helps you to become even more expert as you make explicit what works for you, and why. When analysing practice, working collaboratively is helpful, enabling us to share experiences, learn from others and celebrate successes as well as move on from our mistakes. We are able to think about what values are being promoted by our behaviour;

however subconsciously. Understanding what we do, why we do it and the consequences of that action is the best way to improve practice. What matters is the quality of the learning experiences we provide.

In addition to the central importance of positive relationships, valuing self-esteem and believing we can make a difference, a teacher must also plan for learning.

## Encouraging appropriate behaviour – your plan to maximize learning

- Know all the pupils and know what interests and motivates them.
- Be consistent about standards.
- Help pupils to own their rules and to understand why they are necessary.
- Praise, praise and praise.

It is difficult to envisage a teacher going into the classroom not knowing what is to be achieved in terms of the curriculum. Similarly you need to be clear about your learning objectives in terms of behaviour. What will the children be able to do, know or understand as a result of your teaching?

### *Organizing the class environment to promote appropriate behaviour and attitudes to learning*

Your classroom provides the context in which learning takes place. It is important to prepare the classroom environment, since the physical organizational factors will influence the pupils' learning and behaviour.

Look at your teaching area and examine the following four factors.

*1. Class layout*
- Is the room attractive and welcoming? Is it a place in which you would want to spend a double lesson or even all day?
- Does it look cared-for? You can often tell the effectiveness of schools by the state of the pot-plants! Take a look: how is *your* spider plant?
- Is there freedom of movement for you and the pupils?

- Is the furniture arrangement suitable for work to be done? Can the pupils work alone and together as necessary? Do you alter the groupings to fit the task in hand?
- Are you able to see everyone? Are you able to teach the whole class together?
- Does your classroom enable left-handed pupils to work effectively? Are they able to sit on the left-hand side of a shared table so writers are not working against each other, or does your room have a left-handed desk-chair?

## 2. Resources organization

The way you organize the resources can help or hinder your attitudes and behaviour.

- Does your teaching area support independent learners? Could a new pupil find everything they need, from pencils and scissors to the listening centre? Could they return the resources without help?
- Are you sure that all the resources are checked and in working order?
- Is there easy access to equipment, with no bottlenecks when pupils go to particular areas?
- Do your displays stimulate work, celebrate work, motivate and act as a centre for resources?
- Are the resources displayed fully used? Are books just there to make a good display or do they support learning? For example, are the pupils directed to certain pages through cards inserted in the book? Are pupils expected to add their thoughts and comments about the text to help others?

## 3. Support structures and routines
- Do the pupils start work as soon as they enter the room? Do they know what to do? Do they start the school day at a challenging pace with your high expectations driving them?
- Do the pupils know where to sit? Do they know what to do? Do they have a challenge to respond to, work to complete, or new things to investigate?
- Is the start of the day pleasant and purposeful?

- Is your time and each pupil's time fully used?
- What are you doing when the pupils come into the room? Are you ready to receive them and talk with them? Or are you dashing about preparing, organizing resources, putting up a display, drinking coffee or marking work?
- Can the pupils choose when to come into your room in the morning?
- How long do the pupils have to wait for your response?
- Do they have something positive to do while waiting?
- Do they know what your expectations are if you are teaching and therefore unable to respond to their problem immediately?

---

### REFLECTION

Susan didn't like maths; in fact she hated it and would opt out of maths sessions, choosing to opt in again when the activity changed to something more acceptable for her. How would you respond?

You could choose to let her opt out, thus reinforcing the unacceptable behaviour.

You could insist that if she chooses to opt out, she should then ask to be allowed back, thus creating a joint decision.

You could work together, out of the heat of the mathematical moment, to establish her perception of how you could help her, rehearse her behaviour next time maths is expected, set targets for future behaviour and establish a corresponding and negotiated reward system.

---

### POSITIVE LEARNING ENVIRONMENT TIP 4

Don't lose teaching moments. For example, if you let the pupils get away with something, it is more difficult to reclaim the situation, i.e. if you talk over their noise, the pupils will perceive that you accept it as appropriate behaviour.

*4. Your strategies*

- Do you avoid blaming the whole class? Remember: whole-class rewards for achievement have a positive effect on individual learning, but whole-class sanctions for the behaviour of an individual have a negative effect on the group and the individuals.
- Do you avoid nagging?
- Do you offer threats you don't mean or can't carry out?
- Are you fair in your treatment of the pupils and are you consistent in your approach?
- Are you a good role model? Are your expectations of the pupils and your actions consistent? Do you push into the lunchtime queue or do you wait? Do you say 'Please' and 'Thank you' to the pupils?
- Do you ask the pupils for their views on the organization of the classroom?

---

**REFLECTION**

- How successful is your organization of the pupils' work and resources?
- What are the consequences of your organization for pupil behaviour?

---

## Learning and teaching

- Do you emphasize the interactive nature of learning and seek to support pupils gaining greater control over their own learning?
- Do you value the learning opportunities provided by mistakes?
- Do you actively support their behaviour?
- Do you choose the most appropriate teaching method? Open-ended, intellectually challenging, problem-solving approaches are a high risk for pupils who need structure and direction.

**REFLECTION**

What is your aim as a teacher?

'To create an orderly classroom in which pupils can learn and can behave reasonably and politely'.

Or 'To be able to deal successfully with disruption or defiance'.

Vision is important: 'If you don't know where you are going, that is where you'll end up'.

What are your strategies to achieve your purposes?

### Minimizing inappropriate behaviour and handling the consequences constructively

As we discussed earlier, the 'ABC' approach to learning is a useful starting point when we want to reduce the occurrence of inappropriate behaviour. Reflecting on the antecedent, the actual behaviour and the consequences of the behaviour helps us to understand the problem.

### A: Antecedent

The antecedent shapes the context in which the behaviour occurs. We need to ask the question 'What is happening prior to the behaviour?'. The way you organize the resources can help or hinder your attitudes and behaviour.

Who is involved? What is the situation? Where does the behaviour happen? What are you, the teacher, doing?

### B: Behaviour

What we can observe is important. What is the pupil doing in terms of observable behaviour? What are *you* doing?

### C: Consequences

What happens next? What are the consequences of this behaviour for the pupil, for other pupils and for you?

In this ABC approach we seek to identify aspects of the teaching environment which we can change, to support the pupil's learning. Teachers who use this approach are able to look for patterns in behaviour and analyse situations where certain behaviours happened. Table 2.1 describes one teacher's evaluation of a challenging situation. The left-hand column describes the process, the right-hand column is the teacher's evaluation of Ashok's behaviour.

| Process | Practice: e.g. Ashok's behaviour |
|---|---|
| **Antecedents** | |
| What happened before the problem behaviour? Was the pupil set up by others? Was the pupil provoked? Was the pupil told off? | Ashok was on-task, well able to complete the work in time and working with interest. Unacceptable behaviour when the teacher announced that there were 10 minutes left to finish work before the plenary and then lesson end. No other pupils were involved. |
| **Behaviour** | |
| Where did it happen, and what else was going on? Alone/with others? Playground/class? Lesson? | Ashok was off-task, interfering with other pupils and their work. |
| **Consequences** | |
| What did you do? What did other adults do? How did the other pupils react? | Teacher stopped Ashok's break time to complete work. Pupils reacted by saying 'Not again Ashok'. |
| How often does this behaviour occur? Is there a pattern? | Daily before every break |

Table 2.1

Looking for patterns enabled the class teacher to see that Ashok really needed support at break time; he couldn't make friends and didn't understand what was expected of him, so he avoided the situation in the only way he knew how: by not going out at break time. The consequences of missing break were exactly what Ashok wanted and therefore reinforced the inappropriate behaviour instead of preventing it.

Once the teacher had understood the reasons behind the behaviour she discussed with Ashok why the school had break times, discussed his feelings about these times and acknowledged how difficult they must be for him. They discussed various solutions. Ashok decided that letting certain fellow pupils in on the problem would help. The teacher discussed, with two other pupils chosen by Ashok, how Ashok found it difficult when he didn't know the games others were playing and didn't have particular friends to be with at break time. It was agreed how these pupils would help Ashok at break time, and agreed that all three should regularly meet with the teacher to discuss how the plan was progressing. The teacher ensured that all staff knew of the targets to ensure Ashok was treated fairly and consistently.

The consequences of these actions were that Ashok was happy to leave the security of the classroom at break time, and the inappropriate behaviour stopped.

---

**POSITIVE LEARNING ENVIRONMENT TIP 5**

- Remember it is the behaviour which is unacceptable, not the pupil.
- A new day should be a new start.
- Create win–win situations, so there is no loss of face.
- You need to get rid of the audience if you are handling consequences.
- For the pupils to want to behave, there has to be something in it for them.
- Avoid using provoking questions 'Why did you . . . ?' which are often impossible for the pupil to answer. 'What did you . . . ?' is a much better way forward.

---

### The power of praise

Pupils try to deliver what their teachers want, but they need to know what that is. Many teachers spend a lot of time emphasizing what the pupils *shouldn't* be doing instead of focusing on what they *should* be doing: what you want and what you praise must be synonymous.

Go back to your learning objectives. If your objectives relate to the process of imaginative writing, why do you praise the handwriting or presentation, both verbally and in written feedback? The pupils should be aware of why you think something is good. If you qualify your praise, other pupils as well as the individual can learn from the comments. So if you tell the pupils they are good, say *why* they are good. Avoid saying things like 'You were really good today', which is an ambiguous statement. Pupils who find behaviour, learning or the class situation difficult need more praise than sanction. Effective praise should be supported with appropriate non-verbal behaviour. Say it and mean it.

## Key skills of preventitive behaviour

Bill Rogers (1998) has developed a comprehensive and very practical approach to positive behaviour, and we would recommend his work.

### Peer negotiation

If you play judge and jury, you create a win–lose situation and the pupil does not learn about how to solve conflict. Bring the pupils together to discuss how they see the problem, how they feel and to work out an acceptable solution. Your role is to listen, fine-tune and reinforce good practice. The pupils need to be taught the skills they need to negotiate such a solution at a different time, out of the emotion of the immediate problem. If the pupils are unable to do this, you give a consequence: 'If you can't resolve this together I will . . . '.

### Modelling

An adult or another pupil demonstrates, with the pupil's permission, what happens and what behaviour is expected in a similar situation. For example, they could consider what happens when you get angry. Modelling what happens to your hands, to your face and to your feelings will help the pupil to recognize the signs of mounting anger. If you model how it feels for the pupil, again at a time away from the emotion of the situation, the pupil will be able to recognize when they feel that way and practise what to do when it happens again.

### Practice

It is very important that you give the pupils new patterns of behaviour and the opportunity to practise them. Pupils should know what their targets are and be given the opportunity to rehearse this new, acceptable behaviour. Strategies should be established to give the pupil space when the situation is repeated. Where do they go? How do they reflect on the situation? What are your expectations of the consequences? You should encourage a goal to aim for, with achievable, recordable targets and a negotiated reward.

---

**PRACTICAL REFLECTION**

Donald was 10: he threw chairs when he was upset. The class teacher took time to model the feelings that led to the chair-throwing, and rehearsed new behaviour for when those feelings were experienced again – which included arranging time-out procedures with the headteacher. Donald agreed for the teacher to discuss with the class how they could support Donald in his targets. He negotiated what his reward should be. Donald had a clear view about what he wanted when he achieved the target behaviour. He wanted his mum to receive a letter of how well he was doing in controlling his temper. He wanted this because he knew his mother only ever received bad news from her children's schools. In small steps, and with a lot of teacher and headteacher commitment, Donald made progress, both with his temper control and with his learning.

---

## Contracting

This is a valuable strategy, especially for pupils who recognize they have a problem and want to help solve it. Early goals must be realizable. The criteria are clearly defined, so all know what is involved and the consequences are also clearly specified. Contracts are always written and signed and should last for a short time, for example a week, in order to allow for revision.

## Reframing

When pupils 'awfulize', for example 'Everyone hates me, no one will play with me', they need support to reframe their thinking, showing the pupil that there is little evidence for this thinking. This self-downing has been described as 'psychological junk mail', and pupils who are prone to it are less effective in their coping abilities and therefore find themselves in trouble.

---

**POSITIVE LEARNING ENVIRONMENT TIP 6**

- Help the pupils make rules which recognize the rights of all in the community.
- Make sure that the pupils know what they are meant to be doing and are responsible for how they choose to behave.
- Good relationships are essential.

---

This chapter has established a framework for creating a positive context for learning and establishing systems to prevent inappropriate behaviour. This doesn't always work, and the following chapter considers what to do if it doesn't.

# 3 Managing difficult situations

*Barbara Gray*

Challenging behaviour can be described as

- any behaviour which prevents the pupil or other pupils from learning;
- behaviour which endangers the pupil or others;
- behaviour which is inappropriate for the age and level of the pupil's development;
- behaviour which isolates the pupil from others;
- behaviour which demands too much from individual staff members or too many resources;
- behaviour which causes the pupil to have a negative self-esteem.

While it is always more effective to prevent problems than to deal with them after they have happened, this is often not possible. So what can we do if we are faced with a difficult situation before our prevention strategies are working? What corrective actions help us to address problems when they occur?

A school community should have a definition of what they consider to be challenging behaviour in the context of that school. Staff

---

**MANAGING DIFFICULT SITUATIONS TIP 1**

- Know what your school behaviour policy states.
- What do you understand to be 'good' behaviour and 'unacceptable' behaviour?
- Is this consistent with the views of your colleagues?
- The pupils need a consistent and fair approach.
- Know what issues the school policy raises for your practice.

should describe and list behaviours which they find challenging. You will recognize that there are many different approaches to these behaviours, and the policy, ethos and context of your school will affect how you respond to challenging behaviour.

## Managing challenging behaviour – immediate strategies

Some of the situations require you to plan ahead; for example if you need to give the pupil time out of the classroom, what support and assistance is available for you? Are your expectations clear, and are there established rules for the class?

### *Encouraging appropriate behaviour*
- Be clear about your expectations.
- Teach appropriate behaviour and skills.
- Praise appropriate behaviour/targets reached.
- Involve the parents.
- Use other people in school to recognize achievement.
- Use rewards.

### *Discouraging inappropriate behaviour*
- Be clear about expectations.
- Teach appropriate behaviour and skills.
- Use effective reprimands.
- Loss of privileges or rewards.
- Involve the parents.
- Separation from peers.
- Use sanctions.

Behaviour management is an emotional issue; it affects what you say and what you do. When you correct a pupil, their response will relate to your behaviour towards them. Be aware of your tone of voice and body language. Maintain a calmness and security for the pupil by an unruffled, assertive use of your voice. Slow your speech down, lower the pitch of your voice, and speak calmly and clearly. Remember to make reference to the class or to the school's rules and rights. If you make a rule-related reprimand you will be making clear your expectations and spelling out the consequences of the pupil not meeting those expectations. This approach should be used when a pupil's behaviour threatens your lesson but does not pose a threat to anyone in that lesson.

- Get the pupil's attention, saying their name before the instruction: 'Sally, this is a warning.'
- Refer to the rule: 'Our agreed rule is to work quietly.'
- Specify the consequences: 'If you choose to disturb the others with your talking, you will have to leave the group.'
- Return immediately to the activity, giving praise to the rest of the group: 'Susan and Paul, well done for continuing with your work.'
- If the pupil behaves appropriately, wait for a few minutes then praise the desired behaviour.
- Never repeat a warning.

---

**MANAGING DIFFICULT SITUATIONS TIP 2**

Remember:

- to treat pupils as they want to be treated;
- to address the behaviour, not the child;
- to act quickly and manage the correction in the least intrusive way;
- to be consistent in your approach;
- to tell the pupil what is unacceptable about their behaviour and what they should be doing instead;
- to find at least three things to praise the pupil for, before being negative again;
- you are not a failure if you need to ask for help.

---

## Behaviours which cause teachers most stress, and what to do

The following behaviours are those which cause teachers most stress. The interventions are those used by teachers working in the context of their schools. We describe strategies which you could consider in the context of your teaching environment.

### Violent behaviour

- Your first priority is to stop the aggressive behaviour. If you have a pupil who is often violent, make sure that you know what to do and where to get help. Don't wait until it happens.
- Stay calm.
- Avoid confrontation and try to defuse the situation.
- Give clear instructions to the aggressor and to the other pupils.
- Enable a time-out for the pupil to regain control and manage the pupil's return to the class.
- If you are worried, send for help.

After the event create the opportunity for the pupil to reflect on the behaviour, what led up to it and the consequences of the action. Get the pupil to talk about how the victim feels and how you or the others involved can support and help. Make sure the pupil knows that this behaviour is not acceptable and why it isn't.

Talk with the other pupils to create understanding in the group. Teach the pupil how to handle their violent temper and to consider their options for behaving in a different way. Involve the parents. Work on preventitive strategies:

- Encourage positive reinforcement.
- Set daily goals with achievable targets.
- Monitor, evaluate and prevent.
- Use a behaviour chart for rewards, involve the pupil in evaluation of behaviour/day.
- Involve other pupils – encourage co-operation.
- Ensure a balance in attention-giving, ignore non-targeted behaviour if appropriate.

### Swearing

Some pupils will not have the social skills to know when swearing is inappropriate. First, therefore, you should ascertain the situation. If you hear conversational swearing, usually outside the classroom, remind the pupils of the school approach to positive language. For swearing caused by frustration, it may be enough to acknowledge the pupil's feelings, give a rule reminder and follow this up with a one-to-one chat later.

When swearing, or other language, is used defiantly or abusively you must be careful not to create another source of conflict. This could happen if you react angrily, demonstrate embarrassment or shock, if you make comments about the pupil's home or draw attention to the situation for all to hear. Rather, try to defuse the situation; will humour help?

- Quietly remind the pupil of the rules and why the language used is unacceptable.
- Assertively express how you feel. None of this should surprise the pupil, since you will have already established your expectations.
- Remind the pupil of the consequences of their action if the behaviour continues.

Be aware that if you react through anger, the message you give is 'I am the teacher, I can't lose.' This creates a losing situation for the pupil and your demands and threats back the pupil into a corner, a no-win situation, which fuels the aggression. Aim to maintain a situation where both of you are winning. If you give a clear choice, the pupil retains the responsibility and both of you are in a winning situation.

### Defiance
- Give the pupil time to think.
- Be clear about your expectations.
- Be consistent.
- Remove the audience and discuss the event with the pupil in a one–one situation.

### Pupils not being where they should be
- Remind the pupil of your expectations, of what they should be doing and where they should be.
- Analyse why it is happening. Is it due to boredom, to lack of resources, to ineffective room organization or to inappropriate planning?
- If this is a frequent problem, negotiate achievable targets and rewards.
- Monitor and record progress.

### Inappropriate talking and shouting

- Establish what is acceptable and make sure the pupil understands the expectations.
- Evaluate the organization of your room in relation to the problem.
- Give clear instructions.
- Explain why it is necessary to work in silence or more quietly.
- Be clear about the consequences of continued behaviour. For example: 'If you continue to . . . you will have to . . .'.
- Stop the pupils and set targets.
- Achieve them.

Longer-term measures could include the introduction of a self-regulatory system. For example, in a primary school the pupils could monitor their own noise level and use a noise-level gauge to indicate to the rest of their group if changes are needed in a particular activity. The gauge would have a movable arrow which the pupils use to show the noise level for their group. The rest of the group would be expected to respond (see Figure 3.1).

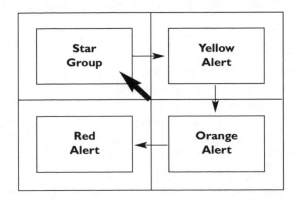

Figure 3.1

### Managing anger

Many pupils are unable to express their anger, so they make sure we know that they are angry by their actions. In response to this you can

- speak calmly but firmly;
- give clear, brief instructions and reminders of the rules;
- use time out of the class if necessary (colleague back-up and assistance is vital for this approach);
- rehearse recognition of physical changes before the aggressive act and rehearse alternative strategies;
- acknowledge that it is not wrong to feel angry. What is important is what the pupil does with the anger;
- set targets and establish rewards.

---

### MANAGING DIFFICULT SITUATIONS TIP 3

- It is vital that after any situation of challenging behaviour you make time to follow up the event.
- When the pupil is calm, talk through the incident. Discuss the situation with the pupil after the heat of the moment. Don't forget to listen.
- Re-establish your relationship with the pupil.
- Set targets for changes in behaviour.
- Work with the pupil to develop a plan of how that pupil will deal with the situation next time. The ideas in the 'modelling' section of the previous chapter should help.

---

It is important to establish listening systems for pupils to be able to express and share their feelings about behaviour. Circle time, thinking books and special pupil times are three ways to achieve positive listening times, which can be adapted for any age group.

*Circle time*
As we suggested in the previous chapter, this is a group listening system which enhances self-esteem, enables reticent pupils to participate and provides opportunities to promote moral values and social skills. Views can be discussed, issues of behaviour debated, consensus agreed, solutions worked out and action plans devised. Pupils have the opportunity to develop the following skills:

- listen, think, look, speak, concentrate;
- to be honest about their feelings;

- learn to respect others' points of view;
- recap and reflect;
- express what others can do to support their learning.

### Thinking books
Thinking books, or personal journals, are tools in which pupils can reflect. They can share them when they choose.

### A time for each pupil to be special
This works effectively as a book, poster or card where the class contributes positive comments about the pupil. It can be part of a circle time, when all are asked to say why that pupil is special. The written forms have the advantage of permanence for the pupil to celebrate their worth later and to share with their parents.

As teachers we know that some of the pupils bring with them problems which cannot be solved in the classroom. The causes are beyond our control and we cannot always provide solutions. But we can always offer respect, support, concern, understanding and encouragement. We can always maintain clearly defined, high expectations for pupil behaviour.

# 4 Voice management

## *Graham Welch*

## Why is voice important?

Consider these three examples of voice use in a school setting:

> Jane was a primary school student teacher in her final year. She was regarded as an outstanding prospect by her tutor. Her planning was thorough, interesting and appropriate to the needs of her final teaching practice class. Despite this, the children's behaviour became a cause for concern as the practice progressed. The tutor observed that Jane spoke with a distinct 'edge' to her voice and considerable visible neck tension.
>
> For over two years, a secondary school choral conductor's high soprano voice had gradually deteriorated. She spoke and sang with severe hoarseness and very limited pitch and volume range. She felt that her career as a teacher was threatened.
>
> A voice educator presented a programme on voice skills to a class of 10 and 11 year olds. He noticed that one child had a noticeably hoarse voice quality when she spoke and sang. He suggested that the teacher recommend an examination by a voice-ear-nose-throat doctor and the school speech-language pathologist. The teacher was surprised and said that making such a recommendation had never occurred to her. When the parents were contacted, they said that the girl always had a hoarse voice, and they thought that her voice was supposed to sound that way.

In the first example, the university's voice specialist enabled Jane to become aware of her underlying vocal tension and to adopt strategies that changed her vocal behaviour. She passed her practice and began a successful teaching career.

In the other two examples, both teacher and child were examined by interdisciplinary voice teams who also took extensive medical and vocal health histories. The teacher's team concluded that the condition of her voice was greatly influenced by a hyper-extroverted personality and her wide-ranging professional commitments. The teacher required surgery and voice therapy, followed by reconditioning of the tissues and muscles involved in producing her voice. Although her soprano capabilities returned, the greatest challenges were in changing the lifestyle choices that precipitated the condition: numerous professional commitments *versus* personal restoration time, voice use *versus* voice recovery time, and her eating and sleeping patterns.

The child was also treated successfully through a course of voice therapy (with no surgery) that addressed the long-standing dysfunction and remedied the physical basis for her condition.

These are examples of the nature of voice dysfunction that are increasingly common in the world of education. Not all voice problems will be so long-standing, nor severe enough to warrant surgery and therapy. But there is a growing body of evidence to suggest that voice management is a critical element of successful teaching.

## Teaching, voice use and misuse

In the last five years, there has been an increasing recognition of the importance of voice in the world of work. Apart from the obvious cases of actors, singers and broadcasters, new research evidence has demonstrated that salespeople (including travel agents and telephone marketeers), clergy, social workers, lawyers and counsellors all rely on voice as a 'primary tool of trade'. In particular, teachers require a healthy voice to undertake their work in the classroom. However, they are also one of the highest 'at risk' groups. The current research data from across Europe (including the UK) and the USA have revealed the following:

- Teachers are 'professional voice users'; voice is a 'primary tool of trade' that is necessary for them to undertake their work successfully.
- However, as an occupational group, teachers have the greatest incidence of voice disorders, making up one in five (20 per cent) of patients attending specialist clinics.

- Twenty per cent of teachers surveyed reported that they missed between one day and one week of work per year because of their vocal conditions.
- In two major European studies, over 50 per cent of teachers stated that their voice had been a problem at work in the past year because it did not function adequately.
- Twenty-five per cent of these had problems daily for weeks or months.
- The most frequently cited vocal symptoms were hoarseness, vocal breathiness, weakness, tiredness, effortfulness and a low-speaking voice.
- Teachers with voice disorders are often found to spend the most time on activities that are vocally demanding.

In addition, related research studies in Northern Ireland, USA and Scandinavia have indicated the following:

- Female teachers more frequently report a voice problem, even when teaching subjects similar to male teachers.
- Women had a higher average number of symptoms compared to men, particularly for younger age groups.
- The teaching of physical education and working in a nursery were associated with increased vocal risk (irrespective of sex).
- Voice disorders can accumulate with increasing years of teaching.
- Many teachers are likely to persevere without seeking specialist help, despite having a recognized problem.

So, overall, many more teachers than workers from other occupations report difficulties with their voices, and their voice problems are more frequent and more persistent.

One of the reasons for the relatively high incidence of voice disorders among teachers relates to the nature of the physical environment in which they work. Although the dangers of noisy environments to hearing have been widely documented, it is only recently that evidence has emerged about the similarly negative effects of a noisy environment on voice use. Once again, it is teaching that tops the list of 'high risk' occupations because

- teachers have to use their voices each working day;
- there is very little, if any, recovery time for voice rest between periods of voice use;
- classrooms are very noisy environments, with significant amounts of background noise, making speech recognition difficult.

In nurseries for example, noise levels have been found to vary between the equivalent of traffic on a busy road, to peak levels that are the equivalent of pneumatic drills! It is not surprising that up to 100 per cent of sampled kindergarten teachers have reported voice problems.

Unfortunately, the acoustic design of most classrooms (often with many hard, reflective surfaces) is such that both teachers and pupils have to make their voices work harder to be understood. This increased vocal effort also increases the risk of tissue damage, particularly if the classrooms are dry, dusty, over-heated and badly ventilated.

Critically, voices need to be hydrated to function efficiently. The design of the human body is such that it is capable of maintaining its optimum hydration levels by normal patterns of eating and drinking, breathing through the nose (which warms and moistens the air) and voice use balanced with voice rest. Speaking circumvents the normal hydration system (by bypassing the filtering and hydrating effect on the air by the nose). As a result, teachers become more dehydrated and increase the susceptibility of the voice system to damage and disease. So, all teachers need to increase their fluid intakes and then maintain higher intakes than the normal working population.

---

**VOICE HEALTH TIP 1**

Keep hydrated; drink at least seven 8 oz glasses of fluid a day, including plenty of water.

---

## How the voice works: anatomy and physiology

Essentially, voice is produced as an interaction between the *voice source* (the larynx) and the *voice resonators* (the vocal tract). Air from

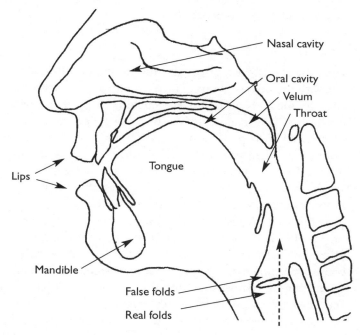

**Figure 4.1**   Lateral view of the head and neck showing principal voice parts

the lungs streams through the larynx, setting the edges of the two vocal folds in vibratory motion. This creates pulsed sound waves that travel (mostly) upwards through the physical cavities of the throat, mouth and sinuses to be radiated outwards from the lips. We perceive this sound as human voice (see Figure 4.1, where the upward-pointing arrow indicates the direction of the airflow from the lungs).

The *voice source* is the larynx which contains two sets of muscles that have the prime responsibility in the production of voice pitch and loudness. The interaction between the two sets of laryngeal muscles contributes to our aesthetic perception of voice quality (such as breathy, edgy, mellow or flutey).

The *opener/closer* set of muscles in the larynx is responsible for keeping the vocal folds apart (as in silent breathing), for moving them close enough together so that their edges can vibrate in the airstream (as in speaking and singing), and for keeping them firmly pressed together and shut tight (as when swallowing food and drink) to ensure that the airway remains clear.

Do this:
- Put your hands flat together in front of you (as in prayer), but with the fingers pointing forward rather than upwards. Keeping the ends of the fingers touching each other, open the heels of your hands. As you look down, you should see an inverted 'v' shape. This is what your vocal folds look like from above when you are breathing silently and not speaking (or singing). The pointed tips of your touching fingers are the front of the larynx. In adult males, this lanryngeal prominence is often called the 'Adam's Apple'.
- Now bring the palms and heels of your hands back together so that they and your fingers are just about touching each other. This is the shape of your vocal folds from above when you are speaking (or singing). You must imagine that the air is streaming upwards from your lungs (below your hands) and flowing between them, gently creating a slight vacuum between your hands so that the skin on your two palms is drawn together, then pushed apart, then drawn together again, and so on. This movement equates to the vibration of the vocal folds. In normal quiet conversation, your vocal folds vibrate in the air stream approximately 250 times per second (female) or 125 times per second (male), being one octave lower.
- Now press your hands together hard! Imagine how much more difficult it would be for the air to push between them now. This is the action of the vocal folds when you eat and drink, creating an airtight seal to stop food and fluids entering your lungs.

The opener/closer muscles are mainly located at the back of the vocal folds near to the spine. As well as assisting in basic vocal fold vibration, this set of muscles is also involved when you change the loudness of your voice. If the closer muscles are fully activated and the opener muscles are relaxed, your vocal folds are kept tightly closed together. It now requires much more effort from the airstream to push them apart. Eventually, because the muscles that activate your lungs are bigger and stronger than those in your larynx, it is usually possible to get some air between the vocal folds. However, the effort bursts the folds apart and then snaps them back together, creating a bigger disturbance of the air, which is perceived as a louder voice.

So speaking loudly requires more effort and is produced by stronger collisions of the vocal folds. If prolonged, this effortful collision can create tissue damage in the vocal folds and will, at least, produce swelling.

---

Do this:

- The muscles that bring the vocal folds together are set in an 'x' at the rear of the larynx. Make the inverted 'v' shape again with your hands in front of you, with the heels of your hands apart. Now imagine that the closer muscles are creating an 'x' shape in the space between the heels. When these muscles are activated, they shorten in length and bring the open ends of the vocal folds together. When you make loud-voiced sounds, these muscles are required to work very hard.

- Tap the back of one hand lightly with the other. Do this a dozen times and listen to the sound it makes. Now increase the effort so that it is more of a 'slap' on the back of the hand. Do this a dozen more times and listen again. Now hit the back of your hand very hard for a further dozen times and listen again. Did you notice that the sound got louder with each set? Imagine talking loudly to a class for an hour. This would equate to nearly a million hard slaps on the back of your hand! No wonder that some teaching situations threaten vocal health! And notice how the skin on the back of your hand began to hurt!

---

The *lengthener/shortener* set of laryngeal muscles is essentially responsible for pitch change. One set of muscles within the vocal folds themselves is the 'shortener' muscles. These have a horizontal orientation (front to back – see Figure 4.2). When these contract, the

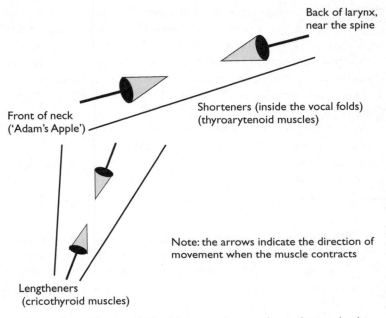

**Figure** 4.2    The lengthener/shortener laryngeal muscles involved in vocal pitching (viewed from the left side)

result is a fatter, bulkier vibrating tissue that produces a lower pitch. Conversely, the task of the 'lengthener' muscles is to stretch the vocal folds and, in so doing, raise voice pitch. The lengthener muscles have more of a vertical orientation and are attached near the front of the larynx (see Figure 4.2).

The effective action of each of these shortener or lengthener muscles requires that the other is 'switched off' (= less involved), otherwise too much combined muscular effort is required and voice quality (health and longevity) is affected adversely.

When your voice gets louder, the 'closer' muscles are activated and so are the lengtheners and shorteners. There is increased airflow to create the louder 'snap' of the vibrating vocal folds and so your lengthener/shortener muscles have to work harder to resist the airstream and function normally. This means that louder voicing involves many different muscles and widens the potential for muscle fatigue.

*Voice resonators* is the term used to refer to the physiological struc-

Do this:

- The reason that we use the term 'vocal folds' rather than 'vocal chords' is that they are three-dimensional; they have vertical as well as horizontal dimensions. Put your hands together in the inverted 'v' shape that you made earlier. Slowly peel your hands apart from bottom (little finger) to top (thumb); this is one vibratory cycle. Now make the same movement, but this time make the pattern only with your top two fingers and thumb. Notice that the contact area is less than when you were using your whole hand. When your vocal folds are stretched, they become thinner and the contact surface is less. As a result, the vocal pitch is higher. Now make the movement with your whole hand (all fingers peeling apart) again. Here, the vocal folds are relaxed and fatter. So the contact surface is much greater. As a result, the vocal pitch is lower. Men have larger vocal folds than women, so their voices are naturally lower in pitch (larger contact area = lower voice pitch).

- Roll up your sleeve so that you can see your upper arm. Hold your arm out straight in front of you. Slowly bring your forearm upwards. Notice what happens to your upper arm. The muscle bulks and gets bigger, that is, as the muscle shortens, it gets larger. If this were your larynx, your voice pitch would get lower as the vocal fold muscle increased in size. Now slowly stretch your arm out horizontally in front of you. Notice what happens to your upper arm. The muscle gets smaller and thinner. If this were your larynx, your voice pitch would get higher. Remember, muscles cannot elongate themselves; they can only contract. If they are to be elongated, another muscle must contract whilst the original muscle relaxes. In the case of your arm, there are muscles on the outside of your arm that relax as you bring your arm up, then contract as you stretch your arm out.

tures above the voice source, specifically the vocal tract, which is the 'tube' that connects the voice source (the vocal folds) to the lips (see Figure 4.3). Acoustically, this tube can be conceived as having several elements or chambers. Each of these chambers individually and collectively interferes with the sound waves initiated by the vocal folds to create particular voice qualities. With the tongue also modifying the spaces in the mouth and upper throat, it is possible to create a complex variety of different sounds (such as those we perceive and label as vowels). The overall effect is to shape a unique vocal output for each individual that is capable of being measured as a 'voiceprint', in much the same way that each finger has its own unique fingerprint.

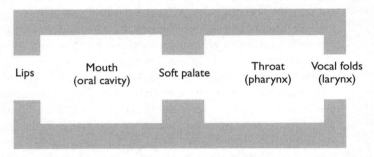

| Lips | Mouth (oral cavity) | Soft palate | Throat (pharynx) | Vocal folds (larynx) |

**Figure 4.3**    Key elements of the vocal tract (viewed from the left side and straightened out from Figure 4.1)

So, vocal sound is *generated* by the vocal folds in the larynx and *modified* by the vocal tract through altering the dimensions of the vocal tract. Various muscle groups allow us to *lengthen* or *shorten* the tract, as well as *constrict* or *expand* it. Ideally, optimum voicing is produced by maximizing the available spaces and ensuring that the larynx is in a relatively low position for a lengthened vocal tract (compared to the 'at rest' position).

Do this:
- Experience the sensations in your vocal tract as you say the following with different voice qualities. Count backwards from twenty in your normal speaking voice. Now imagine that you are very tense, tired and irritable. Count backwards again from twenty with great impatience! In contrast, now imagine that you are trying to rock a baby to sleep. Count backwards from twenty in a soothing, relaxed and restful manner.
- Experience the changing shapes of the vocal tract as you hum in three different ways. First, say the word 'Mum' and sustain

the final 'm'. Now say the word 'Under' and sustain the 'n'. Did you notice the difference? With the 'm' your lips were closed; with the 'n' your lips were open. Now say the word 'among' and sustain the 'ng'. This time you should experience a more open jaw and the sound coming from the back of your mouth, near the soft palate.

These two exercises demonstrate some of the ways in which the vocal tract can be shaped. In the first, the voice qualities shifted from 'normal' to 'constricted' (= narrower spaces and shortened vocal tract), to 'relaxed' (= larger spaces and lengthened vocal tract). In the second exercise, the three hums were created in the front, middle and back of the mouth by shifting the tongue.

Do this:
- Stand in front of a mirror so that you can see your mouth and neck. Repeat the two exercises above and see how your feelings from your vocal tract correlate with the visual feedback. Can you see the changes as well as experience them? Notice that some of the changes that you feel are not so obvious to the eye because you can only see the outside of your vocal system, not the inside. That is why it is important to *feel* what is happening.
- Say these vowels out loud: A, E, I, O, U. Now stand in front of a mirror and say them again. Look at how your mouth and neck might be involved. But is all this change necessary? Make a round 'oo' shape with your lips. Now say the five vowels again, only this time try to keep your lips in the same shape. If this is tricky, it is because the front of your mouth is used to doing all the work when you speak, rather than making best use of the other muscle groups that surround the rest of the vocal tract. With practice, you should be able to keep this mouth shape (or any other that you choose) whilst varying the shapes internally. You should be able to feel how much the tongue and throat are sometimes constricted and so need to be exercised like any other set of muscles.

Finally, be aware of the muscles in your *neck*. Make a point of looking at the necks of different speakers (and especially actors and actresses on the television). You will notice that some speakers have very relaxed necks, with no obvious signs of tension. Others will speak with vertical bands of muscle standing out (such as one famous female character in *Coronation Street*), indicating that their vocal muscles are having to work too hard.

---

Do this:
- Find a colleague who is willing to assist with your voice development. Ask them to stand next to you at an angle of 90° so that you can observe their stance from the side (as in the orientation for Figure 4.1). Ask them to count backwards from twenty out loud and observe the alignment of their spine as they are speaking. Are they upright, or is their head tilted slightly (forward, backward)? If necessary, adjust their alignment by gently moving their chin and observe what happens to the voiced sound and to the muscles of the neck. Are there better or worse positions? Then ask them to observe you while you do the same exercise. How does their visual feedback relate to what you felt as you were speaking? (You can always use a video camera to record the vocal behaviour for repeated analyses.)

---

The head is very heavy and the muscles of the neck have to work with extra effort if it is out of alignment with the spine. The optimum alignment should have an imaginary vertical line traced from the crown of the head (at the back) down through the neck, shoulders and arms. Anything that resembles a curve in the spine when speaking is misaligned and will involve the muscles external to the vocal tract being overly involved, resulting in unwanted vocal tension (because the other muscles used in voicing have to tense more to compensate for the misaligned head).

> ### VOICE HEALTH TIP 2
>
> When speaking, feel your spine lengthening; keep your eyes forward and knees relaxed.

## How the voice works: psychology

You *are* your voice: your voice *is* you. It is an essential element of your self-identity; of who you are and of how other people experience you. Your voice conveys your inner state to the outside world. Whether you are depressed, sad, stressed, nervous, happy, relaxed, friendly, or confident, each of these inner feelings will be reflected in your voice quality. Even on the telephone, when voiced sound is filtered and only part of the real vocal sound is transmitted, you can almost instantly tell the mood of the speaker at the other end of the line, particularly if they are well known to you.

Long-established vocal behaviours can sometimes be difficult to change because they are habitual. Furthermore, such change can be perceived as very threatening to the individual, because any modification of your voice quality is an alteration to how you perceive yourself and the habitual way that you present yourself to the outside world. In certain cases, a particular voice quality is a product of long-established inner tension, and remedial therapy to change these vocal behaviours can have a dramatic and cathartic effect by releasing such tension (resulting in tears or even momentary physical collapse).

For a teacher, this knowledge is important, because the converse is also true: if you want to change your mood (for example, to convey an inner purpose and strength), then deliberately speaking in a particular manner can effect such a change. You can also affect the mood of others. Your voice conveys messages to your audiences in other-than-conscious ways in addition to the intended meaning of the language used. For example, think about how you would say 'Hello' to someone you disliked, compared to someone you loved. The word is the same, but the underlying message and meaning could be quite different.

Often teachers only consciously recognize how powerful the voice is as a professional tool when it goes wrong and does not work as they intend. In order to motivate, assist, empower, enable, as well as teach pupils, the *medium* (your voice) has to be in step with the *message*. Student teachers sometimes discover that all their careful lesson preparation is ineffective (as with Jane) because the essential means for conveying the planned lesson, their voice, displays contrary messages (such as stress, tension, anxiety, a lack of control, irritation, even anger). Even when other aspects of managing the learning environment are all satisfactory, inappropriate voice use can disrupt the intended learning outcomes.

## How to look after your voice

Vocal health, like any other aspect of health, requires good habits. You can assist your vocal health by adopting voice protection behaviours, such as in the way that you use your voice and by your choice of food and drink.

### *Voice resonator protection*
- Keep your spine in a vertical position, with your eyes looking forward (rather than upwards) when you speak, particularly to large groups such as a whole class or school assembly. There should be a 90° angle between the line of sight and the vertical alignment of the spine.
- Allow your larynx to be in a relatively low position when speaking (and singing). Practise being aware of your low larynx position by touching the front of your larynx (your Adam's Apple) as you speak (and check with a mirror). With a relatively lowered larynx, your voice should sound mellower, warmer and more relaxed. This should also have a beneficial effect on your pupils' behaviour.

### *Voice source protection*
- Always try to avoid hard attacks when speaking. This minimizes the vocal folds being pressed hard together and then having them burst apart by the airstream. (It is equivalent to the difference between clapping your hands together gently or hard.)
- Speak with your voice more on the breathy side, rather than with an 'edge' to it.

- Whenever possible avoid coughing and shouting as both of these involve heavy collisions of the vocal folds.
- Avoid speaking for long periods in noisy situations (including some restaurants and clubs where there is a lot of ambient noise) as this can encourage bad voice source habits. In noisy environments the vocal folds have to collide with greater force for you to make yourself heard. This additional force can cause swelling. In a classroom, particularly (but not only) with younger children, adopt strategies to attract pupils' attention other than shouting above their noise.
- If you cannot avoid speaking loudly sometimes, always allow yourself sufficient voice recovery time afterwards. So, lessons/learning activities that involve vocal effort should always be counterbalanced with relative quiet and voice rest, both for teacher and pupils.

### Your environment
- Avoid speaking in dry, dusty environments. If necessary, use a humidifier in the classroom to keep the air more moist (such as by having a fish tank, or a special humidifying container that hangs on a radiator). Whenever possible, ask your school cleaner to wipe the floor with a damp cloth regularly to keep the dust down.
- Ensure that your classroom (and home) has good ventilation.

### Your diet
- Keep hydrated; drink plenty of water. This is essential if your professional life requires you to use your voice, because you are constantly losing vocal tract surface lubrication through evaporation. This fluid must be replaced each working day to protect your vocal mechanism.
- Avoid consuming food and drink that dries out the vocal tract, such as cheese, milk, butter, chocolate, as well as strong alcohol.
- Do not smoke; avoid speaking in smoky environments.
- Avoid fizzy drinks, including carbonated water, as the ingested gas can allow stomach acids to return upwards and attack the lower edges of the vocal folds, creating severe and sustained laryngitis.

- Do not eat late in the evening, as poorly digested food can have the same effect as the gas in fizzy drinks when you lie down to sleep.

You will hear a difference in your voice if it has been overworked. Take note! In many cases, adopting good voice protection strategies will allow the voice to repair itself within a few days.

---

**VOICE HEALTH TIP 3**

- Educate your pupils about healthy voice use and voice protection. This will also help act as a reminder for you own vocal health!
- Make healthy voice use a habit.

---

*Part Three*

# Success with Colleagues

# 5 Your professional role

*Barbara Gray*

*I think the most difficult thing for me was having to learn quickly with very little support . . . at times you feel you will never pick the job up. However, what I learned is that you must ask for advice when you don't understand. Nine times out of ten the other teachers take it for granted that you know. It's never very long before another new teacher begins in the school and then you begin to feel less useless and far more useful.* (Julie, three years' primary teaching experience)

This chapter is about the choices that we make which can enable us to work effectively with others. This doesn't mean that we have to respond to all of our colleagues in the same way.

Colleagues can be

- friends with whom the relationships continue outside school;
- friends just at work;
- easy to co-operate with in work, but we would not seek their company outside;
- those with whom we would choose minimal contact.

We can't expect every working relationship to be of a friendly nature, but it is reasonable to expect that most people will wish to work co-operatively together. Ways in which this can be encouraged are discussed next.

## Motivators and demotivators

What makes you achieve? What drives you? Are these 'drivers' the same for you as for your colleagues? How do we cope with a situation like this?

> One problem I encountered was to get other staff to see my
> point of view, particularly if they were older or had been in the
> school a long time. (Year 2 teacher)

Some teachers can feel threatened by young, enthusiastic or inexperienced teachers, who demonstrate that they are secure with innovations and imposed changes. These experienced teachers need to feel valued and understood. The newer teachers threaten their self-esteem, and more importantly their status.

Abraham Maslow began to develop a theory of human motivation in the early 1940s, which is still widely regarded as valid. He argued that humans have needs which can be best understood as a hierarchy. If you satisfy a basic need, it will no longer motivate you, and so you move up the hierarchy of motivation. If, for example, our physiological needs for food and water are met and we feel safe then we will be motivated to other things such as

- social needs of love and belonging, for example, feeling a valued part of the school community;
- self-esteem and status, for example, being appointed KS2 leader;
- self-actualization, which is about achieving personal dreams and becoming all you can become.

It's fairly easy to assess our own needs in this hierarchy and if we have a high self-esteem it is easy to be positive about our own achievements. In working out how to respond to colleagues, however, we need to try to evaluate where they are in the needs' hierarchy and discover what makes them achieve. Then when you need their help, you can put your request in ways that appeal to them. You can help them feel good about themselves by being positive about the achievements that matter to them.

Difficulties in schools are often caused by other people behaving as de-motivators, especially through, for example

- gossiping or complaining;
- secret conversations from which some people are excluded;
- resistance to change;
- unwillingness to support each other;
- silence in meetings, but lots of discussion afterwards.

You may not be in a position to modify the de-motivating behaviour of others, but you do have choice in your own behaviour:

- Will you join in this behaviour in order to feel part of the group?
- Will you be assertive and explain how you feel about supporting any proposed change?
- Will you hold on to your own positive approach and values when negativity reigns in the staffroom?

## Emotional awareness

The more understanding we have of ourselves, the more we are able to understand our effect on others and them on us. We need to recognize our emotional state, to recognize our attitudes, values and beliefs. We need to recognize how others affect our perceptions, our thoughts and our behaviour. Do you:

- recognize which emotions you are feeling, and why?
- know the links between your feelings, and what you think, what you say and what you do?
- know how your feelings affect your performance?

---

### PROFESSIONAL PRACTICE TIP 1

Find a colleague who is a soul mate, someone who shares your views, someone who will support you in your values, someone to give you the courage to stick with what you believe. At the very least this should be someone who will be a supportive listener when the demotivators seem overwhelming.

---

## Communication

Once you have an idea of what motivates your colleagues, your communication techniques can be adjusted to fit these needs. There are basically four different positions we can choose to take. These tell us what we think of ourselves and what we think of others:

1. We are both winners.
2. I lose, you don't.
3. You lose, I don't.
4. We are both losers.

Table 5.1 highlights these positions and identifies the type of communication that will be evident, the type of learning that will be possible and the source of conflict in such situations.

| | What will the conversation look like? | What sort of learning will be evident? | Will there be conflict? |
|---|---|---|---|
| Winner–winner | Both participants will be open and communication will be easy. | Both people will be willing to learn from the situation | No, since both will avoid conflict by seeking clarification and negotiating a mutually beneficial solution. |
| Winner–loser Loser–winner | The 'loser' can be defensive or aggressive or may have a tendency to be self-downing. | Learning is usually obstructed, only taking place if the loser's need for reassurance is met. | Possibly, as the loser will blame others or reject the ideas of others. |
| Loser–loser | Both participants will be hostile. | Participants are unwilling to accept responsibility, and want to delegate upwards. | Definitely, the conflict increases and other people will be involved. |

**Table 5.1**

Successful communication is easiest when all the participants strive to understand, to be perceptive, to aim for clarity and to demonstrate self-confidence.

### Self-image

Life is not always perfect and communication with colleagues isn't always successful. Moving towards this position is easier if both parties have a good self-image.

Starting any new post, whether it is your first or fifth post, can be a potential threat to your self-esteem. You become more secure as you experience a year in that school context, behave in ways that are familiar to you, and know what is expected of you. These components should help you to achieve this security.

*Flexibility*

Are you able to change your mind when faced with new information? Or do you become tense and irritable when, for example, you have to change a lesson timetable?

*Empathy*

Are you able to feel what the other person is feeling and able to communicate that feeling? This requires listening to feelings not just words.

*Being positive*

Children identify easily with their teacher's mood. If the teacher is cheerful and optimistic and doesn't become upset in the face of problems posed by children or colleagues, then classrooms are likely to be happier.

*A sense of humour*

It is important to keep a sense of perspective, being able to laugh at ourselves and of not being too emotional in a situation.

**Assertiveness**

Self-esteem is an important part of being assertive. Assertive behaviour aims to achieve what you want from others without affecting their rights, demotivating them, or building walls through negative communication.

Which of these would you classify as assertive behaviour?

- 'I feel upset when I am asked to do so many things because I know I will not have time to prepare them properly.'
- 'You are always giving me extra things to do without much notice. You ask too much of me.' (See Professional Practice Tip 2.)

Assertive behaviour communicates:
1. *The expression of positive feelings.*
   - How do you receive compliments? People are often more threatened by being given a compliment than giving one. Answers such as 'It was nothing, that's what I am paid for' are self-downing. 'Thank you, I worked hard on that' is an assertive answer.

**PROFESSIONAL PRACTICE TIP 2**

Assertive statements

- begin with an 'I' statement which includes your feeling about the situation;
- then make a 'when' statement;
- end with a 'because' statement.

The first statement is assertive because using 'I' demonstrates your ability to express your feelings. 'When' qualifies the occasion when you feel this way. The 'because' statement demonstrates that you have a logical reason for your feeling.

- When was the last time you gave an unprompted compliment, without an ulterior motive?
- Are you able to make requests? This is a sign of strength, not weakness, and demonstrates your ability to accept that you don't know everything.

## 2. Self-affirmation
- Are you able to stand up for your rights? If someone changes something to which your response is 'That's not fair', what do you do?
- Are you able to say 'No'? We are sometimes manipulated into doing something we don't want to do because of our self-talk; for example, we talk ourselves into something we don't want to do because of guilt.
- Silence always indicates consent. Are you able to express your opinion, especially when you disagree with the majority?
- Are you able to restate your position if necessary?

## 3. The expression of negative feelings
- Can you express justified displeasure and annoyance? We demonstrate assertiveness when we develop and use the skill of being tactful when criticizing.

- Are you able to express anger? We need to develop the skill of expressing extreme feelings without being aggressive. This is usually achieved when we express how something makes us feel, rather than beginning with 'You . . . '.
- Are there groups of people in school with whom you are able to be more assertive? Is it easier with those of the opposite sex, with support staff, your peers, or your leaders?

---

**PROFESSIONAL PRACTICE TIP 3**

To become assertive you need to develop the skills of

- calmly repeating what you want. This helps you to avoid being distracted by irrelevant issues from the other person;
- calmly acknowledging that criticism of you may be justified. If you do not instantly oppose the disputant's outburst it is possible to separate personalities from problems;
- actively seeking constructive criticism from others;
- asking for and listening to another person's solutions to your problems;
- proposing a negotiated solution to a conflict so no one loses face;
- using 'I–when–because' statements.

---

*Practise your assertiveness*

In teaching we encourage pupils to rehearse their actions in order to enhance their ability to tackle real situations. Likewise rehearsal can help us too. Practise how you would approach these situations assertively using the examples in Figure 5.1.

*Decision-making and problem-solving*

Assertive communication, which successfully motivates yourself and others, needs to be underpinned by your decision-making and problem-solving skills.

*How would you assertively tell a person you are too busy to talk?*
If for example you have your day carefully planned with every moment accounted for, but your headteacher wants to discuss a new initiative with you today.

Feeling (I . . . )

Behaviour (when . . . )

Effect (because . . . )

*How would you admit you are wrong?*
For example, if you discover that you haven't carried out the proposed targets set for a pupil, and now is the time to write a report for the next review.

Feeling (I . . . )

Behaviour (when . . . )

Effect (because . . . )

*How would you ask for information you need from a leader?*
For example if your curriculum leader/head of department is busy but has promised you the details of an intended curriculum change which you need now for you to have enough planning time.

Feeling (I . . . )

Behaviour (when . . . )

Effect (because . . . )

**Figure 5.1**

---

### PROFESSIONAL PRACTICE TIP 4

- Try 'people watching' so that you learn from the behaviour of others.
- Identify aggressive, assertive, passive and manipulative behaviour. Notice how different approaches affect the behaviour of the participants.

Consider a challenge which you have to meet; for example; planning a class field trip, or how you will use your new classroom assistant effectively, or achieving improved differentiation of tasks for different groups. Then follow this decision-making route and reflect on how it works for you (Figure 5.2).

| The route | Your example |
| --- | --- |
| **1. Define your problem**<br>• Consider the facts.<br>• How does the problem look to others? What are their opinions, prejudices and values?<br>• Is it a problem or an opportunity?<br>• How is it affected by the school culture?<br><br>**2. Analyse the problem**<br>• Is the problem solvable?<br>• Do you need to take action?<br>• Will school policies or procedures help?<br><br>**3. Think of solutions**<br>• Be creative.<br>• Brainstorm solutions without evaluating the quality.<br>• Make 'For' and 'Against' lists.<br><br>**4. Prioritize solutions**<br>• What is to happen?<br>• Sort priorities according to: time, resources and people to support.<br><br>**5. Sequence tasks and identify roles**<br>• When and where is it to happen?<br>• Who is responsible?<br><br>**6. Implement your plan**<br>This is the 'doing' stage.<br><br>**7. Evaluate**<br>How will you know if your solution has worked? What will be the criteria for success? Evaluation will lead you back to Stage 4 or Stage 1. | |

Figure 5.2

## Seeing things from the headteacher's point of view

Headteachers have feelings just like everyone else on the staff. Usually, but not inevitably, they

- have been promoted because they can lead people well and have good interpersonal skills;
- will consider the needs of colleagues, pupils, parents and governors before their own needs;
- will be more skilled than you are at motivating, communicating, promoting self-esteem and problem-solving;
- will respect and value you and provide good advice and support.

*But* they also have off days when problems seem insurmountable. They may have great successes in areas other than interpersonal skills and can sometimes fall short of 100 per cent effectiveness in personnel relations. If this is the situation you are in, what can you do?

- Try to understand and empathize.
- Be positive about yourself.
- Approach another colleague about your problem, request, suggestion or idea.
- Talk with colleagues in other contexts to discover what is possible.
- Use your mentor or other leaders in school to support your needs.
- Use the processes in school, such as appraisal and professional development target-setting, to make your support needs known.

---

### PROFESSIONAL PRACTICE TIP 5

Reflect on your abilities:
- What are your strengths and weaknesses?
- What are you doing about them?

Watch others:
- What are their strengths and weaknesses?
- What do they do to build on strengths or overcome weaknesses?

---

# 6 Your place in your school

*Derek Bowden*

A key element in your success is the way you fit in with your colleagues. In this chapter we consider the issues raised by working with others, differences in attitude towards the job, seniority and status, the culture of the school and the demands of teamwork.

## Understanding your job

Your job consists first of tasks and responsibilities that make up your *legal contract*. Second, there are the things more difficult to define but which make the difference between being an *adequate* teacher and a *good* teacher, e.g. commitment, goodwill, enthusiasm, enjoyment, imagination, excitement, humour. These are the ingredients of the buzz perceived in those classrooms where there is quality. You are not paid for them; you choose to give them. They make the *psychological contract*. They can best be summarized in the words of one teacher as 'generosity of spirit'. Teaching is a job where you give of yourself throughout the day (and often evening). That is why it is exhilarating (and exhausting).

What do you and your colleagues put into the psychological contract? Note your three main contributions in Figure 6.1 and compare these with how you perceive others.

| You | A colleague | Your headteacher |

Figure 6.1

You can probably identify colleagues who fulfil a major psychological contract and others who keep it to a minimum. These different perceptions of our jobs are the source of many tensions and conflicts among staff in schools. It is not easy to have productive discussions about, for example, ways of dealing with a problem pupil if some participants see themselves as responsible only for what happens in *their own* classrooms. A person who will only do what is in their job description (working to rule) can affect both the range of activities and the community atmosphere of a school. Beware, though, of the headteacher or colleague who thinks that your generosity of spirit is infinite so that you can always be approached with requests to take things on. Your enthusiasm can become exhausted and you have to learn to say 'No'.

## Understanding your professionalism

What motivates you to teach? Yes, we all do it for the money, we have to eat and the rent must be paid. But if it's only for the money, you are probably in the wrong job. We need long-term motivators, the things that make a job worthwhile despite the occasional 'Monday morning' feeling. These are recognition, belonging, achievement, and empowerment.

*What motivates you?*

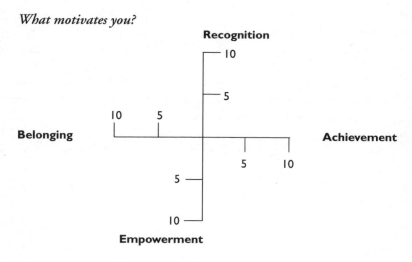

Figure 6.2

Mark your rating of yourself on each axis in Figure 6.2. A score of 10 means:

- *Recognition:* 'What I do here is known and acknowledged.'
- *Belonging:* 'It is made clear to me that I am an integral part of the school – I belong here.'
- *Achievement:* 'I succeed in most things and am making progress in others.'
- *Empowerment:* 'I am given space and authority to make decisions, to get things right and, sometimes, to make mistakes.'

*High scores:* your ideal profile is four '10s'. This means you are working as a full professional in a professional climate, that you have opportunities to lead, to collaborate, and to follow. You are proactive.

*Low scores* on any axis mean you are restricted in your professionalism. Low scores on all four indicate problems; you are working as an operative, i.e. you see yourself as doing what you are told. You are reactive.

Increasingly teachers are seeing themselves as reactive operatives. Much of this derives from draconian political attitudes towards education and from legislation which draws power away from schools towards central government. There are also schools where the management style, by treating people as operatives, can reduce the professional space of their teachers. Beware, though, the danger of allowing yourself to become a victim, of blaming others. High scores on the motivation profile are not given to you by others – your own actions, attitude and approach to the job can influence greatly the way you are treated, perceived and perceive yourself.

---

**PROFESSIONAL-WISE TIP 1**

Behave like a professional and use the guidance given in this book to increase your chances of being treated like a professional.

---

## Understanding your status

Our society is status-conscious. You have probably already met a variety of reactions when you respond to 'What do you do?' 'Teacher' as a label does not attract awe and respect, and teachers tend to collude with this. Examples of status ranking abound.

'I'm just a *reception* class teacher' – from someone introducing herself at a course.

'I'm only a *primary* head' – at a conference of headteachers.

Perhaps the best, from a further education college staff wine and cheese evening, by a (male) head of department introducing a new (female) member: 'This is my *assistant* colleague.'

Prejudice is alive and well in our society and is reflected in the experience of a former colleague who found that some men were daunted by the prospect of going out with a female physics teacher, so she would describe herself, instead, as a teacher of children.

Status is reflected in the way many schools define their organizational structure as a pyramid, with the headteacher at the top, standard-scale teachers at the bottom, non-teaching staff in a margin, and pupils nowhere in sight. You might like to suggest at the next staff meeting that the pyramid is inverted so that the learning interaction between teachers and pupils is at the top and all other aspects support this core function (but do not expect promotion if you do!).

How do people of different seniority and status relate to each other in your school? This reflects the culture (the hidden dynamics) of the way the school operates and the way you behave similarly to fit in.

- Is a boss–subordinate relationship apparent in body language, tone of voice or formality of dress?
- Do you find yourself being patronized or are you listened to as carefully as any member of staff?
- Are first names used equally?
- Do non-teaching staff attend social functions?
- Will people openly disagree with the leader?
- Is the term 'junior staff' ever used?

Look at your school's formal published policies, aims (mission), structures, and processes. Compare these with what actually happens. There are schools whose publicity proclaims 'a caring community' but the experiences of pupils and staff do not necessarily reflect a caring ethos. We have seen charts of consultation and meeting structures in schools where staff feel decisions are made irrespective of views expressed 'from below' and that the meetings held are paper exercises. We must also say that this is balanced by an increasing awareness on the part of school managers that a consumer-conscious public expects the school to do what it claims to do.

This 'iceberg' model (Figure 6.3) gives a useful frame for looking at your school's organization.

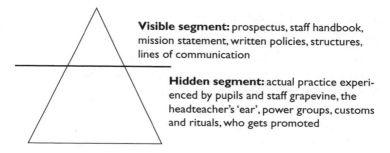

**Figure 6.3**

When the two segments are aligned, this is the sign of a healthy organization.

How would you represent your school using this model?

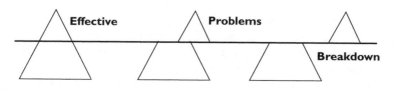

**Figure 6.4**

School managers have to deal with massive pressures in today's educational climate. They sometimes concentrate on the false security of administrivia and written policy in the top segment, allowing themselves increasing distance from the day-to-day matters being dealt with by the staff, in the hidden segment.

> ### PROFESSIONAL-WISE TIP 2
>
> The more you understand the workings of your school, the better able you will be to work in comfort within its culture, and, as a professional, influence the school.

## Understanding your teams

Cutting across a school's structure are numerous teams. You will be a member of one or more teams. In a small primary school, perhaps the whole staff can be regarded as a team. In a larger primary there might be Key Stage teams. In a secondary school or college there will be departmental teams, perhaps pastoral teams. In any school there can be specialist working teams like heads of departments, curriculum development groups, and the senior management team.

Most people regard teamwork as a good thing, and many advertisements now specify 'team players'. Management texts and staff handbooks accept that effective teamwork is the key to a successful organization.

Hidden within all the team hype are interesting issues.

- Teams usually have leaders, so we are back to the conundrums of power relationships.
- Compared to being a subordinate where you are answerable to the boss, if you operate within a team you are accountable to all its members; they all depend on you.
- It is assumed that people automatically have team skills, yet teamwork requires high-level abilities. A proactive professional will learn the skills of teamwork; a reactive operative will wait to be told what to do.

Think of a specific team to which you belong. Use Figure 6.5 to assess the members' skills.

Be realistic: in statements 9 and 10, for example, even in the most established teams, people could probably not score 10. All of us have some personal private territory. Realize also that in statement 18 (which is a vital component of teamwork) 'critically' means

*Skills of effective teamwork*    *Score each statement between 1 and 10.*
*1 = absolute NO; 10 = unreserved YES*

| PURPOSE AND DIRECTION | 1) I feel we have a sense of purpose | |
|---|---|---|
| | 2) I know where we are going | |
| INTERACTION AND COMMUNICATION | 3) We communicate well within the team | |
| | 4) We know what is happening around the school | |
| DECISION-MAKING | 5) We make clear decisions at the right time | |
| | 6) When decisions are made, we act on them | |
| PARTICIPATION AND LEADERSHIP | 7) I am involved in policy and organization matters | |
| | 8) I am supported and monitored in the quality of my work | |
| OPENNESS AND TRUST | 9) I feel comfortable to speak openly | |
| | 10) We can disagree without hurting personal feelings | |
| USE OF TIME | 11) We concentrate on important issues | |
| | 12) Our time together is well used | |
| ABILITIES | 13) The tasks I am allocated match my interests and abilities | |
| | 14) The distribution of jobs within the team is fair | |
| FLEXIBILITY | 15) We plan ahead to be ready for change | |
| | 16) We can be flexible to meet different situations | |
| EVALUATION | 17) We regularly review our progress and effectiveness | |
| | 18) We talk critically to each other about the quality of our work | |

**Figure 6.5**   Assessing the quality of teamwork

positively as well as negatively, i.e. 'The way you did that was brilliant' is a criticism; it is an evaluative statement.

### Risk takers' variation

The insight is increased if several or, better, all members of the team complete it. It identifies areas where the team is effective and areas that need improvement, but if more than one person is involved there is a risk of filtering the responses to avoid offending each other. If you do it together you must *explain* your assessments to each other with evidence and examples. From this shared assessment an action agenda for team development can be created.

So, you didn't score highly on all the qualities of teamwork? Were any of the following the causes?

### People barriers

- *The awkward person:* often referred to as a 'strong' character, as a euphemism for self-centred and negative.
- *The defensive person:* the 'dinosaurs' who like things to remain as they are and will resist any change.
- *The stirrer:* those who enjoy 'rocking the boat'. It can be constructive but often is derived from resentment of other people's success and progress.

### Organizational barriers

- *Too big:* above six to eight people the team dynamics change so that fully collaborative work becomes less easy.
- *Overload:* common in today's target-setting, league-table, OFSTED-driven climate. Be prepared to identify and address priorities and shelve the rest. Good strategic planning is vital.
- *Tasks not completed:* a common response to overload and the failure to prioritize.
- *All talk, no action:* another response to overload brought about by lack of leadership and poor decision-making. Each decision needs an implementation action plan.
- *Lack of autonomy* : the team needs to know what authority it has and must ensure that responsibility is matched by authority to act. This is linked to clear delegation from senior management.

- *Sense of isolation*: determined by the relationship of the team to the rest of the school.
- *Lack of resources*: another product of overload at school level. Make clear decisions about what can be tackled and achieved.

We know teams and schools who have benefited greatly from collectively assessing their team skills and identifying barriers to success. It is risky but it can be fun, and the potential for team growth is enormous. Do not try it as a twilight activity; it needs at least half a day and it helps if you can use a facilitator who is not in your team. A critical mass of the team must be willing to participate.

## Understanding communication

You earn your living as a professional communicator, dealing (amongst other things) with the development of intellect. This seems like a rational process; it isn't. It's much more than that.

You know that the quality of communication in the classroom depends on relationships. If the emotions are OK, two-way communication can work. When the emotions are not OK, the ability to give and receive information is impaired.

The staffroom is the same as your classroom. There are emotional dimensions to every conversation. For example, a simple question like 'Have you handed in the reports yet?' can be taken to mean 'You really should have finished them by now', or 'If there is a problem, let me know.' The way you respond depends on how you interpret the question, the status of the person and whether or not you like them.

If a colleague said 'Those shoes look smart', your response might depend on a number of (non-rational) factors. What do you think of your colleague? The shoes they are wearing? The way they are dressed generally? Do age, gender and status colour your responses?

We use a model to help us understand communication (Figure 6.6). The closer each circle is to *you*, the greater is its effect on your communications.

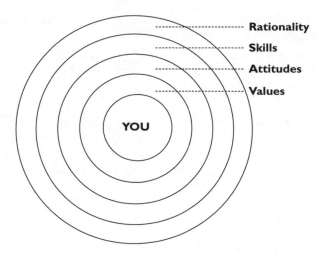

Figure 6.6

- *Rationality*: this is the logical, non-emotional processing of information. However hard we try to be objective and rational (using our outer layer), the way we interact with colleagues, parents and pupils is influenced by a whole range of subconscious, value-driven factors.
- *Skills*: these translate your attitudes and values to apparent rationality. Your vocabulary, inflection, tone of voice and non-verbal signals all play key roles. Similarly, as a listener you employ a range of skills, interpretation, connection and translation of verbal and non-verbal signals.
- *Attitudes*: your feelings about the person, the nature of the message or the situation. We listen 'with attitude'. The way we translate A's message is determined by our feelings towards A. If we like them we are more inclined to interpret the message in the way they intended. What makes us like them? Probably some common ground in attitudes, indicated by appearance, manner, tone of voice, posture. For example, some of us intuitively reject a statement made in a booming 'superior' voice. A soft regional accent will be listened to differently. We are filtering the message through our own attitudes (which are many!).
- *Values*: you hold deep values, sometimes subconscious,

which affect the world-view and from which attitudes derive. Each of us transmits and receives through our personal world-view – our values provide a set of filters. What are your filters? What are those of the person or people with whom you are dealing? How are you influenced by age, status, social class, accent, gender, race, looks, vitality? Do you give everyone the same hearing?

A school community will have a whole variety of world-views built on the rich variety of values and attitudes held by its members. An understanding of these gives insight into the way you respond to people and they to you. Think hard before you comment on a colleague's shoes or ask them about reports!

### How effective is your communication?

Think of particular colleagues with whom you communicate successfully, and those with whom you have a problem. Using Figure 6.7, try to identify the key skills, relevant attitudes and underpinning values which affect you when dealing with them.

|  | Successful | Problematic |
|---|---|---|
| Skills |  |  |
| Attitudes |  |  |
| Values |  |  |

**Figure 6.7**

### Risk-takers' variation

If you want deeper insight, discuss your findings with carefully selected others; some from your successful list, and (higher risk) one or two from the problematic group. Do not ask them about themselves! Ask them about how they perceive you.

PROFESSIONAL-WISE TIP 3

Looking in a mirror is not always a pleasant experience. If you have asked others about your communication skills you have the opportunity, with greater self-awareness, to improve your skills and learn to accommodate your attitudes. You might need to work hard on attitudes which are a real barrier to full professional behaviour.

## Understanding conflict

At bad times the teacher's job can seem to be a constant round of aggravation with awkward colleagues, demanding parents, detached senior management and pupils from hell. To deal with conflicts with these, we need to keep a sense of balance. Remember that our schools are also full of warmth, with friendly, helpful colleagues, co-operative pupils, and supportive parents.

We need techniques, not to avoid conflict but to cope with it, without damage. Most of us have periods when one or two individuals seem to poison the quality of our existence.

The approach you use depends on the nature of the problem. How close is it to you? Is it affecting the quality of your work? Does it affect the atmosphere of the workplace? For example:

- *Distance:* conflict with a close associate whom you meet regularly needs more urgent resolution than a problem with someone meeting with you less frequently.
- *Effect on your job:* you want to achieve quality teaching but your head of department or curriculum co-ordinator is not providing information or resources essential for you to implement curriculum plans. Their response to your repeated requests might be prevarication or 'You don't really need that, make something up yourself'.
- *Atmosphere of the workplace:* a colleague using shared resources leaves things in a mess and you have to tidy up; or a colleague regularly uses your coffee without replacing it.

To resolve conflicts such as these,

- find solutions where both parties feel the outcome is reasonable. If only you benefit from a solution, it can be good for your stressed ego but your colleague has a sense of having lost. 'Remembered pain' is a powerful force and conflict will resurface. Then,
- negotiate within a defined objective which is justified in terms of the school's purpose; it is not about proving anyone right or wrong, or pride, or showing who is in charge.

Bearing these principles in mind, work to the following stages.

### Stage 1
- *Agree a time and place.* Do not catch the other(s) by surprise, and avoid places where there will be an audience. If someone is angry or upset do not go for the quick fix; successful negotiation needs a low temperature.
- *Express your concern.* Confirm its importance to you by setting up a proper opportunity to talk. If, for example, a parent has stormed in, then make a cup of tea while allowing the steam to blow off – it is not worth attempting reason at this stage.
- *Indicate your determination to resolve the problem.*

### Stage 2
- *Understand the other's position.* Reflect on the four factors influencing your colleagues and your own communication (values, attitudes, skills, rationality). To an angry parent, for example, you can represent the hated system of their own employment (or lack of it); their brushes with the establishment (benefits office, council); the baggage of their own bad experiences of school; or the pecking order of their power struggles at work.

### Stage 3
- *Listen.* Give them a chance to explain. Listen without challenge. Seek clarification if necessary.
- *Tell them you understand (not necessarily agree with) their position.*

- *Don't try to justify your own views, nor appear to patronize.* If the issue is about a pupil, that child (whatever you might think of them) is locked into the parent's self-identity. Can any of us be rational, even fair, when our children are in trouble or being badly treated? If all this fails, don't fight. One of the authors was once accused by a parent of keeping his son in detention in order to claim overtime (actually a promising idea!). The father's physical removal of the boy was not resisted, although it did cause problems with the other detainees.

### Stage 4
- *Agree objectives to meet the needs of people (not the system or the rules).* When parents complain on behalf of their children, we need to agree on objectives for the teachers, the child and the parents. Look forward, not back.

### Stage 5
- *Know (but do not state) your bottom line.* Before the discussion, decide what you are willing to concede and what is non-negotiable.

### Stage 6
- *Support opinions with evidence.* When giving opinions and assessments, use evidence based on identified criteria. If you don't, you could have a number of separate conversations which do not actually converge.

### Stage 7
- *Be sensitive to your emotive triggers and those of the other person.* These might take discussion off-course. Be ready to declare 'out of order' personal or aggressive comments, but do so in terms of 'unfair' rather than 'outrageous'. You will often be face to face with people you do not like, whom you distrust, whose value system you abhor. You might feel much the same way about a pupil, but remember the old teacher's advice – 'Deal with the behaviour, not the person', 'Deal with children as what they might become, rather than what they are.'

*Stage 8*
- *Always leave a way forward.* If it is going downhill, avoid failure. Declare 'time out' for a re-think or a cup of tea. It is difficult to express anger while looking over a full mug (unless they decide to throw it at you). Do not allow collapse; always have a way forward. That way you reach win–win.

This eight-stage process takes time, preparation, trouble and skill, but is more cost-effective than numerous, unproductive, bile-raising squabbles.

---

**PROFESSIONAL-WISE TIP 4**

Although our focus in the above chapter is adult–adult negotiation with angry, upset, anxious parents or colleagues, it can work as well with recalcitrant pupils.

---

# The skill of saying 'No'

We noted earlier in the chapter that you, being an enthusiastic and co-operative teacher, are likely to be approached by the headteacher and other colleagues to take on extra tasks. It can be a useful career move to agree, but beware of becoming the 'easy touch' to whom people talk about delegation when they really mean dumping.

You will often be approached in a corridor or busy room. Do not be rushed into a hasty decision. Use the stages below:

1. Ask for a proper discussion with time to think.
2. Find out exactly what is expected of you, the scope of the task, what support is available, and the timescale.
3. Ask what is in it for you. Money is unlikely but recognition, time and professional development are possibilities.
4. Ask why you were approached, and if other people/possibilities were considered.
5. If you agree, do so positively (never grudgingly) but point out that you cannot endlessly take on more work. Confirm the level and type of benefit you will receive and the answers to question 2 above.

6. If you are inclined to refuse, you might wish to ask for time to consider so that you can compose your response. When saying 'No', do not apologise, give the reason(s) for your decision based on not lowering the quality of your current work, and express regret that you cannot help on *this* occasion, and your appreciation of being asked.

*Warning!* If you are in a school where a senior colleague might seek to punish a refusal, it might be sensible to accept so that your track record helps you to get a job somewhere else quickly.

## A personal postscript from one of the authors

On the evening after writing the section on negotiation, my wife and I were being taxied by our 19-year-old son to an evening with friends. On the way he casually commented 'You two drink too much'.

What a wonderful opportunity for a father/son discussion on an important topic using objective criteria as a focus! The reality was, of course, a tomcat slanging match where we criticized each other's lifestyles and claimed superior fitness while my wife tried (and failed) to be the reasonable peacemaker. We all behaved with classic obedience to the stereotypes.

I cannot always reconcile the skills I am able to employ in a work context with my behaviour at home. There, instinct and emotion seem to operate more quickly than rationality and logic. Perhaps I should not try too hard and maybe, with my family, just be my natural self, leaving the cultivated skills to be part of my professional portfolio.

# 7 Significant others

*Angela Thody and Barbara Gray*

## Meet the others

During our initial teacher education, we all learn how to manage pupils. In many cases little attention is paid to managing the many adults with whom teachers interact. Parents, support staff and governors all need recognition and support for the parts they play in children's education, and all of them can make your life as a teacher significantly more successful than it would otherwise be. If your relationship with them is effective, their positive impact will be enormous, though their visibility to you may be slight. If your relationship with them is ineffective, their negative impact will be enormous, as will be their visibility.

## Parents and carers

### Relationships

It is important to understand how parents and teachers react to each other. A group of teachers identified the following, when asked about problems they had encountered at the start of their teaching careers:

> A parent, high on drugs and alcohol, confronted me because his daughter had been criticized. (Rhys, Year 9 teacher)

> Lack of support from parents, particularly those with children who have behaviour problems. (Rachel, Year 4 teacher)

> Having to be the one to tell parents the real academic level of their children. (Gary, Year 2 teacher)

> Irate parents who shout loudly and do not listen easily. (Julie, Year 5 teacher)

The teachers also recognized parents as a source of great encouragement, but as one said 'It is just a shame that most parents wait until you are leaving a school to tell you how wonderful they think you are'. It is, however, important to keep things in proportion. When you are experiencing difficulties with one parent, remember all the parents who think you are effective and developing their children's learning effectively.

Parents are your pupils' first educators. Did you know that we have learnt 85 per cent of our adult language by the age of 5? Parents continue to influence their child's learning, therefore an active partnership with parents is vital. 'Partnership' implies a two-way sharing of knowledge, and awareness. You can begin this process by questioning their feelings and yours about the partnership. Here are some typical responses from parents.

- School is a world where some of the parents failed, and they may be fearful of re-entering it. In contrast, teachers, even the newly qualified, are confident in school.
- Parents don't want their children to have the same experiences of failure that they had.
- Parents want more success for their children than they had themselves.
- Some parents will feel it is their fault that their child is in trouble, others won't care.
- Some parents do not have the self-confidence or the vocabulary to speak to you.
- Parents may not feel welcome in the school.

What do you feel about your pupils' parents? Are they fund raisers, unpaid helpers, experts, co-educators, potential problems, interfering? Your views will affect your expectations and your relationships with parents.

---

### SIGNIFICANT OTHERS TIP 1

View parents as partners in the process of solving your pupils' problems.

### Planned meetings with parents

Formal meetings between teachers and parents need careful preparation to produce an effective process that includes a thorough review.

#### Preparation

- Have all your records to hand.
- Ensure all primary and special school pupils have work displayed. Secondary school teachers should ensure that there are displays of work in corridors and specialist rooms. Parents will feel that their children's work is valued, that their children are seen to be important. They will be able to use waiting time to see the school's standards of achievement.
- Arrange the furniture so parents don't feel daunted; if you use your desk or a table, make sure that the parents have one too. Use chairs of the same size.
- Consult your school's guidelines:
  - Can you use a timer to ensure that you keep to the timetable?
  - What is the procedure for offering extended time?
  - What record of the meeting should be kept?
  - What support will be available if a parent becomes abusive towards you?
- Check that parents can find their way to you. Is your name displayed prominently? Make sure that you can direct parents to other members of staff and to the refreshments.

#### Process

- Welcome every parent as if they are your first appointment that evening – even when they are your thirtieth.
- Speak from your records.
- Visibly take notes during the discussion concerning questions parents have raised, and action points agreed.
- Always start and end with something positive.
- Tell the truth.
- Give parents the opportunity to ask questions and to make comments.
- Follow up parents' concerns and report back to parents.

*Post-meeting review*

- What arrangements were made for those parents who didn't come? Were new dates offered, home visits arranged, or an alternative venue agreed?
- Was the length of time for each parent adequate?
- Were appointment times well synchronized?
- Are you able to vary the way you use meetings? Possible variations are:
  - an opportunity for 'open house' to enable parents to share the work with you and their children;
  - 'early warning' discussions if progress doesn't meet targets or expectations.

In primary schools
  - a meeting at the start of the year with an agreed agenda to discuss the pupil's previous report and to exchange information to assist the settling in to a new class;
  - mid-year discussions centred on work, achievement, potential and learning targets. Parents need the opportunity to read their children's work in advance of the timed appointment;
  - the end of the school year for a discussion based on the annual written report.

In secondary schools
  - a cycle of meetings fitting with the rhythm of key stages;
  - clear explanation of the changes in curricular and assessment arrangements.

---

### SIGNIFICANT OTHERS TIP 2

To write good reports use these words or phrases: 'demonstrated'; 'shown that'; 'needs to change'; 'completed'; 'written'; 'would benefit from'; 'designed'; 'is able to'; 'must now'; 'can achieve'.

Avoid vague statements such as: 'tries hard'; 'could do better'; 'quite . . .'; 'must try harder'.

### Reporting to parents

Written reports are another important part of parent–teacher communication. Analyse your reports using the framework shown in Figure 7.1.

| Good Reporting | Do your reports achieve this? | |
|---|---|---|
| | **Yes** | **No** |
| 1. Sets explicit learning targets | | |
| 2. Involves the pupil in the assessment process | | |
| 3. Reports on the whole pupil | | |
| 4. Includes parents' responses | | |
| 5. Is positive and informative:<br>  – identifies pupil's achievements<br>  – identifies areas of concern<br>  – identifies how parents could support learning | | |
| 6. Is professionally produced | | |
| 7. Motivates pupils to improve | | |
| 8. Is jargon-free | | |
| 9. Is clearly based on evidence | | |
| 10. Balances negative comments with guidance for improvement | | |

**Figure 7.1** Assessing your report-writing technique

## Support staff

### Who are they?

Permanent school staff include classroom assistants, laboratory technicians, information technology experts, dinner supervisors, estates and maintenance personnel, bursarial, clerical and reception office staff. By 2003, these constituted at least one third of the total staff of secondary schools, almost double this in special schools and around half in primary schools.

Some of these support roles will be contracted out to other agencies so there can be a changing panoply of gardeners, caterers, examination invigilators and building workers. And don't forget the school road-crossing wardens and the bus drivers for school transport.

Establishing good relations with all these people means communicating with them – smile, nod, talk about their needs. Make sure you use the nomenclature they accept: collectively, they are variously referred to as support staff, associate staff, ancillary staff, non-teaching staff, administrative, clerical or technician staff.

Any of these titles (especially that of non-teaching staff) can be resented by those who feel they are not regarded as importantly as teachers. In some schools, you will find that all your colleagues are deemed 'the staff' without any distinction being made between those on the front line in classrooms and those who provide other services.

---

### SIGNIFICANT OTHERS TIP 3

Find out as quickly as possible the names and roles of support staff. You can then rapidly access appropriate assistance.

---

### *How do support staff assist your work?*

The numbers, and importance, of state schools' support staff grew significantly from the mid-1980s when schools gained responsibility for almost all of their own expenditure. Like schools in the independent sector, schools had to become financially viable, hence needing to employ more people solely for business management with no teaching responsibilities. This has largely relieved the administrative workload of senior academic staff, but if the school 'business' is running efficiently, teachers at other levels benefit from working in an atmosphere of security. Your managers also have financial information readily to hand to assist them to answer your queries about help with teaching resources. So you gain indirect help with easing your teaching load.

Support staff also lighten your teaching load directly. Since 2003, school support staff should be

- doing bulk photocopying;
- chasing absent pupils;
- collecting money from pupils for school trips;
- ordering teaching materials;
- analysing pupil attendance data;
- copy typing;
- producing standard letters and class lists;
- filing records;
- collating reports on pupils to parents;
- processing examination results;
- setting up classroom displays;
- administering work experience, examinations and teacher cover;
- dealing with ICT troubleshooting and minor repairs;
- stocktaking;
- minuting meetings;
- co-ordinating and submitting bids;
- seeking and giving personnel advice;
- inputting and managing pupil data.

By 2005, support staff will also be responsible for providing all examination invigilation and there are recommendations that they should be used more on educational visits for the pupils outside of school.

All the above are required by national agreement but there are many ways in which support staff can lighten your load informally such as

- keeping parents happy in the reception area until you are ready to meet them;
- ensuring you have your registers each day or that the electronic records are checked for you and you receive information on absentees;
- efficiently cataloguing and enticingly displaying library books in the resource area. Pupils referred from your class can then find your recommendations quickly and feel encouraged to read;
- acting as pupil mentors.

These lists of what support staff do in England's schools can apply anywhere in the world. In many countries, however, schools' administrative, clerical and managerial roles have never been as extensive as those in England as the tasks have been undertaken by local area administrators and/or it has always been accepted that support staff undertake the tasks above.

### Helping support staff

Many support staff feel undervalued and underpaid. Their low pay is a reflection of the pre-1988 situation when most of these jobs were seen as term-time, school-hours jobs for mums. This changed with the introduction of the National Curriculum which targeted the value of employing more and better educated support staff.

Classroom assistants now have opportunities to be certificated and to proceed to diplomas and degrees in education. National training for support staff in England began to be offerred from 2003 with opportunities for teaching assistants to become higher teaching assistants beginning at the same time. For bursars, national qualifications at certificate and diploma level commenced in 2002/3 adding to the specialist MBA for school bursars offered by Lincoln University since 1996. Specialist training is available for most of the other support staff too. Many are now full time and increasingly are needed during the school holidays too. Career ladders are becoming established.

Support staff took over many of the administrative services previously run by the LEAs and are now much more aware of their importance. The more that teaching staff recognize this, the happier will support staff feel and the more likely they are to be extra helpful.

---

### SIGNIFICANT OTHERS TIP 4

- Treat all support staff at least as well as, if not better than, other colleagues.
- *Always* thank them for their assistance.

## Governors

### *Whom are you likely to meet?*

Every English and Welsh school has a governing body. The governors advise and direct the headteacher who is responsible to them for the day-to-day management of the school. In the independent sector, governors are mainly financial trustees and act much like directors of commercial businesses. State schools will have between nine and twenty governors (large schools have the most) as they reconstitute their governing bodies as required by law between 2003 and 2006. The governing bodies will have the same categories of governors as prior to 2003 but with some changes in numbers so they will comprise

- elected teachers (minimum of two, maximum of one third of the total);
- elected parents (minimum one third);
- appointed representatives of the school's principal funders – the Local Education Authorities (one fifth). These are usually, but not invariably, selected by the local political parties controlling the LEAs;
- appointees from a school's founders and funders in foundation schools – business organizations or religious authorities, such as Anglican, Roman Catholic, Jewish, Methodist or Muslim (minimum of two, maximum one quarter);
- co-opted, local community representatives including one from local industry, selected collectively by the rest of the governing body (one fifth in community schools, one tenth in foundation schools);
- optionally, two sponsor governors.

Many other countries have similar bodies, though usually with more teachers and parents. Only in New Zealand do they have such extensive powers and duties as do English and Welsh governors.

### *How do governors influence your work?*

Indirectly and largely invisibly! Their principal activities (usually with senior staff) include the following:

*Set strategic direction and achievement targets and evaluate how far these are reached. Examples:*
- school development plan and budget
- minutes of governors' meetings
- annual report to parents
- audited accounts
- preparation for OFSTED
- post-OFSTED action plan
- school admission numbers and policies

*Monitor teaching, its accordance with the National Curriculum and other government directives, its responsiveness to pupil needs and to raising standards. Examples:*
- meetings of governors' sub-committees
- governors chosen to represent your curriculum area
- special needs governor
- school policies on pupil behaviour

*Management policies. Examples:*
- your job interview/pay negotiations/promotions/redundancies;
- the school's policies on your working conditions and health and safety;
- school policies on professional development and appraisal;
- developments in school marketing and public relations.

*Supporters' club. Examples:*
- governors' visits to your classroom and discussions with you;
- governors attending school plays, social functions and fund-raising events;
- chair of governors dropping in weekly for discussions with the headteacher;
- chair making press statements when there is a school success or crisis;
- teacher governor asking staff for items they want discussed at governors' meetings.

## When are you likely to meet governors?

1. During governors' school visits;
2. At school functions;
3. When you are interviewed for your appointment or for promotion;
4. If you join committees or working parties of staff and governors;
5. During your induction year, you may be encouraged to attend a governors' meeting as an observer (ask, if no one offers this);
6. Participating in elections for teacher governor and standing for election.

## What do you do when you meet governors?

Make them feel very welcome. They are in *your* territory, feeling uncertain. They know little educational jargon or what to look for when observing lessons or assessing your teaching resources. Your practical guidance will make them more useful in governing body discussions, and you will have gained useful friends.

Find out who is your class, subject, year or house governor if she/he hasn't contacted you. Arrange to have a chat if that governor is visiting the school. Ask their advice – it's flattering and it helps you to know the views of those not directly involved with the school.

In joint working parties, make sure you encourage governors to participate in the discussions. Vote in the teacher governor elections. Ask what the teacher governors do.

Occasionally, some governors see their roles as permitting inquisitorial intervention in day-to-day school affairs. In response, overwhelm them with information and with requests for them to, e.g., lead tutor time, attend field trips or help individual pupils. If this fails, then you have to invoke the higher authority of the headteacher or the Chair of the Governing Body to help the governor to recognize where your job starts and his/hers stops.

### SIGNIFICANT OTHERS CONCLUDING TIPS

- Welcome the presence of other adults in your classroom.
- Introduce them to the class.
- Explain what you are doing.
- Find an activity for visitors to your classroom.

*Part Four*

# Success with Yourself

Angela Thody's note: Finding time for life outside teaching is a requirement since 2003 when it became official British policy that 'All teachers . . . should enjoy a reasonable work/life balance' (23, 4, School Teachers' Pay and Conditions, 2003). To help you to achieve this, the government made more money available for support staff so you could be relieved of routine administrative and clerical tasks (see Chapter 7), ordered that you should rarely have to cover for absent colleagues (and only for a maximum of 38 hours per year if it were neccessary) and guaranteed planning, preparation and assessment time within the timetabled working day. So now you have to organize yourself to take advantage of this. Chapters 8 and 9 have techniques to help you.

# 8 Time management

*Derek Bowden*

## Using time well – life outside teaching

Teaching is a busy, pressurized job. Work is not confined to time in school and you, doubtless, spend many hours at home on school-work. This isn't necessarily bad if you are enjoying it, but there is a danger of seeing a 50+ hour week as some mark of noble dedication to the cause of education.

Perhaps working long hours reflects commitment, but it can also mean you miss out on personal and leisure activities. Over the years this can reduce the 'buzz' you bring to the classroom. You can become adequate rather than inspirational. The psychologically tired teacher is the one more vulnerable to stress.

> ### TIME MANAGEMENT TIP 1
>
> Beware joining the ranks of the over-conscientious and unappreciated.

So you would like an evening with three–four hours' free of school-work? Start by using the quiz (Figure 8.1) to identify your personal *time-thieves*.

If you have marked every option as 'Always' then you don't need this chapter. Continue at Chapter 9. If you have options marked in the other columns, consider which of them you could move at least one column to the left. That's the beginning of saving time on work tasks so you can recycle it as personal, family, leisure or home time (your personal agenda), and of making more effective use of work time by prioritizing tasks (your professional agenda).

- The bad news is that to recycle your time, you are going to have to change the way you do things. That can be uncomfortable in the short run.

| | Always | Usually | Sometimes | Rarely |
|---|---|---|---|---|
| 1. I make and use a weekly plan | | | | |
| 2. I am clear about longer-term tasks that need doing | | | | |
| 3. I create blocks of time for big jobs | | | | |
| 4. I deal with interruptions effectively in school | | | | |
| 5. I deal with interruptions effectively at home | | | | |
| 6. I deal with paperwork efficiently | | | | |
| 7. I can find things in school | | | | |
| 8. I can find things at home | | | | |
| 9. I keep on top of marking | | | | |
| 10. I have organized times for preparation | | | | |
| 11. Informal meetings are short and focused | | | | |
| 12. Discussions with colleagues are to the point | | | | |
| 13. Formal meetings in school are well run | | | | |
| 14. I use other people well | | | | |
| 15. Senior managers in school seem to respect my time | | | | |
| 16. The school has efficient systems for routine information | | | | |
| 17. I find time to relax out of school | | | | |
| 18. I programme and maintain my leisure activities | | | | |
| 19. Even when under pressure I feel in control of the day | | | | |

**Figure 8.1**

- The good news is that it really does work: that brings long-term comfort.
- The helpful news is that teams and whole school staffs can collectively attack time management.

The potential benefits are enormous. We recommend that school senior managers accept a key responsibility for seeing that their staff operate in a time-efficient environment. The starting place is to score the statements together to create a *team agenda*. Ways of dealing with these agendas are described in the remaining sections of this chapter.

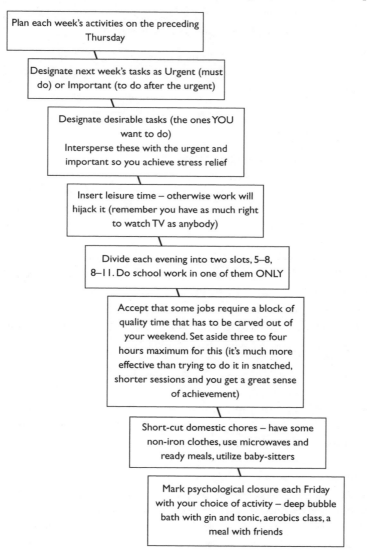

Figure 8.2

All of this is made more difficult (but more necessary) if you have family or domestic commitments. Young children are premier league time thieves, and ironing and cleaning need planned slots. The heavier the commitments, the more important becomes your organization of personal time.

---

**TIME MANAGEMENT TIP 2**

Avoid becoming a victim of the pincer movement between a busy job and other people's needs. Don't feel guilty about prioritizing *your* needs.

---

## Organize your time

### Rule 1: Take control of interruptions

Dealing with a class demands total concentration, which makes interruption of precious non-contact time even more costly to your planning. Interruptions can come from colleagues, children, parents, and other professionals. There are a number of ways of responding to interruptions.

For example, you have one hour free and intend to use the time to start writing end-of-year reports on pupils. These are due in ten days' time but you have very little free time between now and then. A colleague says 'Glad to get the chance to talk to you – we have to arrange those appraisals and I need information on Waynetta for the exclusion meeting next week.' Which of these replies would you make?

- 'I've got to finish these reports now but I can see you at break/after school.'
- 'Can't really help right now – rushed off my feet!'
- 'OK, appraisal first then exclusion. Let's wrap it up in ten minutes, then I'm starting these reports.'

When deciding on a response, you have to balance your needs and priorities with those of your colleagues. It is remarkable how, within a time-aware staff, these assertive responses do not cause offence and the incidence of interruptions is reduced. It is also possible to develop a similar strategy at home; particularly when the task needs a block of time.

**TIME MANAGEMENT TIP 3**

When you can't respond immediately to an interruption, you are not being selfish, you are asking people to respect your time as you respect theirs.

### *Rule 2: Take control of paperwork*

Sort your mail/pigeonhole/tray daily into junk to be binned, trivia to be dealt with quickly (immediately if possible), and important things needing attention. Don't give each piece of paper equal value. You might find the flow-chart shown in Figure 8.3 helpful.

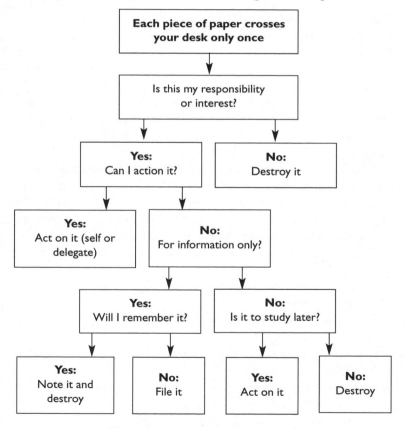

**Figure 8.3** Sorting your paperwork

At school level the management of paper and routine information needs careful thought. A cluttered, rarely-cleared noticeboard is actually a barrier to efficient communication. A named person must be responsible for any staffroom system. Larger schools find a five-minute morning briefing very useful if it is properly planned and conducted. Smaller schools can use a whiteboard in the staffroom with colour coding for topics and/or people.

It is good practice for senior managers who distribute LEA, DfES and similar documents to reduce each to one A4 side of key points, with the original kept available for reference. If bulky documents are just passed on they will not be read. This will only work, however, if staff accept their part of the deal and read the paper.

### Rule 3: Take control of your filing and storage

To begin with we need to analyse the kind of person you are. Are you *the non-filer* ('I know I put it somewhere safe/in this pile/on that chair'); *the hoarder* ('I chuck everything in that box – at least I know I've got it'); *the obsessive* ('I sort everything into classifications, have a box for each when pending, a box for each when completed and then I file all paperwork. I keep everything') or *the office manager* ('I keep only what needs to be kept and have a regular (termly) clear-out. Most of it is electronically filed').

Which should you be? Don't rush to assume that you ought to be the office manager type. The authors have worked with people in all of the above categories. Some manage to be efficient whatever system they adopt; others flounder in stress, trying to find important records even within what appears to be a well-organized filing cabinet.

Organize your filing and storage system so that it

- suits you (you can remember where things are and can access them quickly);
- fits your method of working (clear out once a term, a year, or when moving jobs);
- provides you with enough security that you have retained all necessary documents;
- is within your competence (if you're not computer literate, then electronic filing is not for you);
- meets the needs of colleagues (they don't want their work delayed by your inability to find materials).

> ## TIME MANAGEMENT TIP 4
>
> It is worth investing short-term time into building your filing and storage system for the long-term gain.

### Rule 4: Take control of your marking and preparation

Our experience is that many teachers feel guilty about marking and preparation because they feel they could always do more but there are simply not enough hours in the day.

The purpose of marking is to record achievement and to give useful feedback. Schools are increasingly developing homework and marking policies which highlight the necessity of relevant tasks as well as clear learning objectives (ideally explained to the class). Marking should focus on these objectives. It is a sensible professional strategy to accept that some things will be done to two- or three-star rather than four-star level. Managers should bring this into the open so there is guilt-free dialogue about fairness, priorities and workload; this can prevent the current exploitation by the system of the goodwill (and fear?) of industrious teachers.

To cope with our marking, we have found the advice given in Figure 8.4 useful.

| Pupils' needs | Your needs |
|---|---|
| **Aims of marking** | |
| A sense of achievement. | Awareness of your pupils' progress/difficulties. |
| Useful feedback on how far they have reached the learning objectives. | Avoidance of exposure to the criticisms of well-intentioned but ill-informed parents who feel that insufficient marking is being done. |
| Some indication of the importance of their standards of literacy or numeracy so they are aware that these matter in all subjects. | Ensuring you have enough information for report writing. |
| Rapid return of marked work. | Avoiding exhaustion from trying to keep up with all the marking |

**Figure 8.4**   Aims of marking

**How to mark**

Reduce the red – a mass of comments is demoralizing and the pupil will learn nothing.

Don't correct every error – it doesn't help the pupil to avoid repeating them.

Mark only part of the work for standards of literacy or numeracy; explain why you are including these cross-curricular issues and that your comments are to give an indication of where improvements might be made.

Include positive comments and ticks as well as critical marking.

Check that you are marking in accord with the school's policies on feedback.

Indicate that you have seen each piece of work done by your pupils – even it is only ticked and dated or has a brief comment.

Don't mark every error.

Keep records of your marks.

Feel positive about having completed one pile of marking rather than negative about the other four piles still to be done.

Be aware that marking is to help pupils feel good, and to learn; it is not for senior managers, bureaucracy or OFSTED.

**Figure 8.4**　Aims of marking (continued)

### Rule 5: Take control of meetings

Most staff meetings take place at the end of the teaching (not working) day. A common scenario is of a few people doing most of the talking, with an apparently passive or apathetic audience. Afterwards, in the staff car park, people who have been silent for over an hour break into animated discussion about the meeting. We are concerned that the meeting process fails to channel and utilize this energy and interest. The danger for a young teacher is to assume that 'that's the way meetings have to be'. You might feel powerless to improve meetings in your school but there are aspects the individual can affect. In the following discussion note what *you* can do and what needs to be done by senior management.

First, reflect on what you think are unproductive meetings at your school. How much of the inefficiency do you think is due to the following?

- Meetings lack a clear and generally understood purpose.
- Meetings are too long.
- Agendas are too full, consisting of a list of items rather than a framework for discussion.
- Too many people are present.
- Meetings are run (chaired) by the most senior person present.
- Meetings are adversarial in style, high on structure and formal procedure, low on creativity.
- Minutes of the previous meeting are a nit-picker's paradise, concentrating on the past rather than the present or future.

Each of these problems, and possible solutions, is discussed below.

*Clear purpose*

**Problem:** Many schools are locked into a pattern of meetings decided a year in advance. There are good reasons for this, including the need for people to arrange their diaries. The problem is that the rigidity of structure and, particularly in secondary schools, the various structural levels at which matters are discussed, precludes a fast, incisive response to the unpredictable year ahead. Programmed meetings tend to be held even if not needed. Is there really value in eight different departmental meetings, each discussing boys' discipline? The typical secondary system is so ponderous that the intended flow of ideas up and down the structure is often overtaken by events. We still know of primary and secondary schools where staff have to attend meetings to ensure their 1,265 hours are accounted for. This is a punitive policy which has a negative effect on the goodwill which is the lifeblood of staff relations.

**Solution:** Replace this structure-driven system with a number of small, focused task-groups dealing with specific issues from the school development plan in a short time-frame. The authority of these groups to make decisions or recommendations to senior management must be clearly defined.

*Length of meetings*

**Problem:** Expecting people to contribute usefully for more than one hour after a day's teaching is unrealistic.

**Solution:** Make an hour the maximum and try, using techniques from this section, to reduce this to 30 minutes.

*Agendas*

**Problem:** These tend to contain too many items, forming an unhappy mix of routine administration and deep educational issues. Neither is adequately addressed and items late in the agenda are rushed through or carried over. Each item on the list is given as a single word or short phrase, for example 'end-of-term arrangements'. Let us review this from the point of view of six people attending the meeting. They might have seen the agenda previously, or more likely, have been given it at the meeting.

Andrew: 'This is about closing an hour early like last year.'
Betty: 'This is about having class parties.'
Clive: 'This is about extra supervision at break.'
Donna: 'This is about clearing displays off the walls.'
Edwin: 'This is about having all records up to date.'
Fiona: 'This is about having a collective psychological closure to
　　　promote community spirit.'

Six people will be (partly) prepared for quite different discussions, each of them valid. All might be different from the convenor's intentions.

**Solution:** An active agenda format (see Figure 8.5).

| Item | Item Leader | Purpose | Time |
|------|-------------|---------|------|
| **3. End-of-term arrangements** | | | |
| a) Early closure | Andrew | To identify views on pros and cons for recommendations to governors | 3 mins |
| b) Class parties | Betty | To decide by majority for or against | 1 min |
| c) Break supervision | Clive | To request voluntary staff help for people on duty | 1 min |
| d) Display clearance | Donna | To confirm site manager's request | 30 sec |
| e) Class records | Edwin | To confirm details of necessary records and deadlines | 1 min |
| f) Psychological closure | Fiona | To explain the reasons for and potential value of:<br>• identification of staff views<br>• change of present policy by consensus only | 5 min |

**Figure 8.5**

The agenda should be issued to all participants and displayed in the staffroom (in a dedicated location) for three days before the meeting. It is accepted practice for people with a particular interest or concern to consult the item leader who might then summarize various points as an introduction to the topic. Items (d) and (e) are on implementation of policy and will not be discussed (we know that Fred would like his usual moan about workload at the end of term but we have heard it all before).

## Number of people attending

**Problem:** As numbers rise, the dynamics of a meeting change until spectating and even posturing become more frequent. Observe a large meeting and you will see these and other symptoms of dysfunction. It raises the question of *opportunity cost* (what else the spectators could be doing with their time) and *effectiveness* (the toxic effect of inflexible or defensive views expressed and repeated in front of a captive audience).

**Solution:** Select the number of people according to the purpose of the meeting: 3–6 for explaining ideas and resolving problems; 6–10 for routine management, implementation issues, matters requiring input from particular levels of management; all staff: for quick briefings, for bonding or celebration.

In small primary schools such advice might seem superfluous, but success there lies in restricting the *purpose* of the meeting. With a small staff, it is tempting to have all-purpose meetings which then drag on. Stick to specific purposes and keep the meeting short.

## Leading (Chairing) the meeting

**Problem:** Traditionally this is done by the most senior person present, who is also the convenor responsible for the agenda. The same person is probably the most active protagonist, introducing ideas and fielding questions.

*Solution:* Leading a meeting requires full concentration on the agenda, the participants, the co-ordination of discussion. The chairing (we prefer the terms 'leading' or 'directing') should be done by a member who has co-ordinating, interpreting, and summarizing skills. It is a facilitating role, not an authority/power thing. We suggest that the team leader should (gladly) hand over the responsibility of running the meeting to a colleague. This also sends signals about task-focused collaboration between professionals and reduces the status/power dimension common in meetings.

## Minutes – action report

**Problem:** Minutes are time-consuming and can be inaccurate, inadequate, or superfluous. The business of 'minutes of the last meeting' is a mischief-maker's charter which can be used to undermine the present meeting.

**Solution:** We suggest replacing minutes by an action report which is attached to the relevant agenda. The report lists decisions, the person responsible for implementing the decision, the time-scale and people who need to be informed of a particular item outcome. We suggest copies of action reports to participants with a copy on a dedicated notice board.

---

### TIME MANAGEMENT TIP 5

Start using some of the ideas in this section in small departmental or key stage meetings where status is less of an obstacle. Be patient – they require learned skills.

---

## Use other people's time

This could be subtitled 'delegation' except that this essential component of collaborative work has been mis-used by managers who confuse delegation with dumping. Delegation is a short-term contract with clearly defined tasks, outcomes, levels of autonomy and degrees of supervision. Dumping is a single off-loading of work you don't want to do to someone who can't (or won't) say no.

Delegation, well done, is a massive time-saver. A number of people working individually or in pairs can achieve so much more than by working together through all the tasks. Traditionally, delegation is done 'downwards' in the hierarchy. We suggest you can also delegate 'upwards' and 'across'.

Upward delegation addresses the complaint about senior management frequently heard in the staffroom: 'Why don't they just do it and tell us'. The same people will also complain about 'lack of consultation', but you can't win them all! Upward delegation raises a fundamental philosophical/ethical issue. It involves reducing the amount of consultational participation between senior management and grass-roots staff. The key skill is to reduce the amount, saving many people-hours, but not the level. In this way senior managers can preserve (even enhance) the notion of professional collaboration and valuing colleagues. It requires skilled selection and communication (and occasionally a thick skin!).

Delegation across is essentially a sharing-out between equals. You can also ask a colleague to do a job because they are particularly good at it, or you can offer an exchange of something you will do for them.

---

**TIME MANAGEMENT TIP 6**

Whether colleagues delegate to you upwards, across, or downwards, seek clarification of the terms of the 'contract'. Remind them not to 'snoopervise'.

---

## Senior managers respecting people's time

A time-intelligent school needs senior managers who use their time well and allow/encourage others to do the same. The personal time available to a busy teacher affects the quality of life. We see skilled time management as an *imperative* for managers.

School improvement gained at the cost of the well-being of teachers is short term only. The key is to work smarter, not harder. Too many teachers and senior managers spend time on administration tasks which could be done by a 16 year old.

It is the headteacher, ultimately, who has to take responsibility for many of the strategies suggested in this chapter. Some of them have serious implications for traditional ways of working in schools.

The re-engineering of staff consultation and meetings and the notion of *openly* accepting two- and three-star solutions to workload problems all require brave and visionary leadership.

## Reward your time

### *Relaxing out of school – beware the throbbing bag*
It's likely that you, like us, take schoolwork home – usually preparation and marking. In recent years teachers' bags have become bigger and bigger. Some people now use crates or boxes and need special lifting techniques to empty the boots of their cars! When you get home the bag sits in a corner or under the stairs. Typically, because you are tired from a hard day, you do something else. Maybe you relax within the family, watch TV, or just sit in an exhausted slump. Two hours later the bag is still there and is beginning to send

messages to you. One way of avoiding them is to go to the shops or the pub or watch TV. On your return, it is still there, pulsating. It is too late to start working on it now. The bag goes back to school next day with the work still undone. You will not have properly relaxed the previous evening because of the throbbing bag.

Perhaps you can identify with the scenario. If so, what are the solutions?

- Use the suggestions in this chapter and you will need the bag less.
- Take only *one* job home.
- Remember that you have planned the evening in two parts and schoolwork must only be done in one of them.
- Have at least one evening in the week clear of schoolwork.
- Reward your time.

---

### TIME MANAGEMENT TIP 7

At the end of a homework session give yourself a little reward. These are a key part of time management. It can be a walk in the park, a favourite CD with the cat on your lap, half an hour of rubbish television, or a piece of chocolate (the last one has side-effects – be careful). Identify and look forward to your little reward.

---

# 9  Stress management

*Angela Thody*

---

### STRESS MANAGEMENT TIP 1

You *will* have it all but don't even try to have everything all at once.

---

## The stress argument

Make just one week's trawl through daily newspapers, weekly and monthly magazines for both men and women, and you'll find 'stress' items in every one, with stress perceived as

- a word to use for everything from mild anxiety to severe, clinical depression (if you have the latter, don't spend time on this chapter, go straight to a doctor);
- normal for everyone;
- particularly suffered by teachers;
- always damaging, and we should not be subjected to it;
- preventable with self-help;
- worse now than ever before.

On the other hand, there are the sceptics who feel that stress is just an adult's comfort blanket and it's time we grew up and coped without it. So let's look at the two sides of the argument . . .

## Media hype – stress is everywhere

Headlines tell us that 80 million working days annually in Britain are lost to sick leave for stress. Did you know that 25 per cent of your colleagues are stressed? Every teacher in your school, including you, is estimated to be taking seven days' leave annually for stress-related illnesses (eight and a half days if you are in a primary school). A 2004 report from the USA, found that one third of new teachers leave the profession in the first five years because of stress and 88 per cent of teachers are estimated to suffer from moderate to high stress (www.nea.org/neatoday/0401/stressed.html;09/01/04). This confirms a National Union of Teachers' study reporting in 2000 that stress was the major health concern in one in five schools.

Stress causes you to lose patience with your work colleagues and pupils, forget appointments and fail to produce reports on time. Homeward bound you'll suffer attacks of road rage or supermarket angst. Once home, you'll shout at your partner and/or fall asleep with lack of energy to shout.

The media's suggested cures for stress are legion. From vitamins, to herbal remedies to manufactured drugs – there is a pill to help you cope with stress. Alternatively, why not try physical relief mechanisms such as tapping your head with light percussive movements, power sleeping for eight hours, combing your fingers through your hair, or lying down in an enclosed water tank? Or there's always a professional therapist on hand; in 2003, Professor Furedi of Kent University estimated that there were around half a million counsellors in Britain.

If these fail to help you, go and talk with a relative, a friend, someone at the bus stop, your professional development co-ordinator or even yourself as you stroll a lonely mountain. Start exercising, swim, row, jump, run marathons. Take up a new hobby, study, cook, communicate with your family. All should dissipate your stress.

If you don't have time to fit these in, then use on-site masseurs. These come to your school and chair-massage your stress points. You will be happily back in the work environment in only twenty minutes.

If all these remedies fail, sue your employer and/or take early retirement on stress-related grounds. After all, you did not anticipate having to teach subjects that were not your degree specialism. Nor did you expect that pupils might sometimes be difficult to control or that a parent might be angry with you. Your school should have prevented this happening and then you would not be stressed.

All this stress is apparently only a late twentieth- /early twenty-first-century disease. For teachers, it has been caused by coping with rapid changes in technology, teaching methods, curriculum demands and higher standards to be attained.

## Stress sceptics – pull yourself together

The sceptics see stress as something that has been over-hyped and with which we should be able to cope. A collection of their views includes:

- It's usual for all of us to worry sometimes, but is it necessary to define this as stress?
- Isn't stress something we all need to give us a 'high' to stimulate action?
- A teacher writing in the education press in 1999 complained that he needed one week of the summer holidays to 'wind down' from work pressures. We've heard similar statements from those in jobs with similar levels of responsibility.
- The self-help remedies proposed seem designed to make us more worried as we try to find the time to take the suggested relaxing holidays, do exercises or find new leisure interests.
- Before believing that stress is worse now than ever before, compare yourself with your late-nineteenth-century counterpart. You would have classes of 50 to 60, wages dependent on pupils' results, the demands of a national curriculum, awkward parents refusing to pay the compulsory fees, and annual inspection.
- The stress industry continues to grow by encouraging people to feel helpless because of even minor frustrations such as the photocopier being out of action. Counsellors make people feel they are unable to cope alone whereas we should be learning our own coping strategies.

## Stress busting – a new interpretation

Should we believe the stress hype or the stress sceptics? To resolve the dilemma, we suggest differentiating states of stress as:

distress → anxiety → anticipation → delight

This will help you re-think your attitudes.

- The happy states of anticipation and delight are as much forms of stress as the less happy ones of anxiety and distress.
- Each of these states will affect all of us at some time.
- Each is a necessary, and valuable, part of being human. It is not wrong, or bad for us, to be in any of these states.
- Each time we learn to cope with any of them, we acquire skills that will enable improved coping with subsequent experiences.
- We can regard ourselves as being likely to have difficulty coping only if we face multiple types of distress at the same time or causes of distress over long periods.
- Learning to cope with any of these states can help you empathize with your pupils and be better able to offer them guidance on how to encounter change. Every day, pupils face the anxieties of new aspects of learning, being constantly assessed, having to work with incompatible companions, being required to produce assignments in media with which they are unfamiliar, while simultaneously battling with domestic difficulties.

## Assessing your own distress, anxiety, anticipation and delight

- *Distress:* continuous worrying, feeling sick, panic attacks, inability to act, sadness, waking in the early hours.
- *Anxiety:* occasional worrying, working out every possibility before action.
- *Anticipation:* stomach butterflies, rapid assessment of possibilities before action, looking forward to achievements, quiet excitement.
- *Delight:* joyfulness, exhilaration, satisfaction with actions.

In which of the four states do you most often find yourself? To find out, tick your selected answers to the questions in Figure 9.1.

| | |
|---|---|
| 1. When you first wake in the morning during term time, do you feel:<br>  immediately alert<br>  or still tired? | |
| 2. Do you:<br>  thoroughly enjoy negotiations and discussions with<br>  work colleagues<br>  or find you quickly lose patience with them? | |
| 3. Do you:<br>  relish your reading and lesson preparation<br>  or find it hard to concentrate on them, often needing to re-read? | |
| 4. Do you feel:<br>  exhilarated for no particular reason<br>  or sad with little obvious cause? | |
| 5. Do you:<br>  get started without delay on your work tasks<br>  or keep putting them off? | |
| 6. How would you regard a Friday afternoon coping with an<br>  unexpected double class when there is no supply teacher to cover<br>  a colleague's absence:<br>  as an exciting challenge<br>  or as an unpleasant problem? | |
| 7. Are you:<br>  eating, drinking or smoking as usual<br>  or have you increased any of these significantly in the last twelve<br>  months? | |
| 8. Do you sleep:<br>  soundly<br>  or restlessly? | |
| 9. Do you:<br>  enjoy talking about your work to friends outside your school<br>  or find you are obsessive or frequently complaining about it? | |
| 10. Is your health:<br>  good<br>  or are you suffering from symptoms you don't usually experience,<br>  such as regular headaches, irritable bowel, disinterest in sexual<br>  and personal relationships, feeling dizzy, difficult breathing, heart<br>  palpitations? | |

**Figure 9.1** Assessing your stress type

If you ticked mainly the first box in each answer, then you are experiencing 'delight' or 'anticipation'.

If you ticked mainly in the second boxes, you are experiencing 'anxiety' or 'distress'.

## How do other teachers assess their stress type?

We asked a sample of teachers to answer the above questions so you can compare your views with theirs. Our sample of 42 consisted of those whom media hype most expects to be suffering anxiety and distress, i.e. nineteen headteachers and deputies, seventeen middle managers (e.g. heads of departments, key stage co-ordinators) and six others, including inspectors and peripatetic teachers. They were all at an age to have family responsibilities, and all had given themselves the additional challenge of studying for higher degrees in their spare time.

### 1. Feelings on waking during term time
Immediately alert    19%
Still tired    69%
Others: In between the two; alert in summer, tired in winter or term end; tired at end of term only; tired initially then perk up    10%
No response    2%

### 2. Negotiations and discussions with work colleagues
Thoroughly enjoy    76%
Quickly lose patience    17%
Others    7%

### 3. Reading and lesson preparation
Relish it    42%
Hard to concentrate/often re-read    36%
Others: It gets less time than it should; most done in the holidays; don't relish it but can concentrate    7%
Not applicable/neither/both/no answer    15%

### 4. Feelings
Exhilarated for no particular reason    14%
Sad with little obvious cause    31%

Neither/both    43%
Not applicable/no answer    7%
Others: If depressed or elated, there is always a cause; I don't have mood swings – sometimes get bright ideas    5%

**5. *Getting started on work tasks***
Without delay    48%
Keep putting them off    42%
Both    10%

**6. *Response to the prospect of a Friday afternoon coping with an unexpected double class when there is no supply teacher to cover a colleague's absence***
An exciting challenge    17%
Unpleasant problem    50%
Others: Depends on the previous challenges of the week/on the class; I would consider this as part of what one would do for a colleague – a favour to be returned; as a professional, I would accept it; it's just normal; just a nuisance/inconvenience; light relief    21%
Not applicable/not answered/this could never happen in my school 12%

**7. *Eating, drinking or smoking***
As usual    73%
Significant increase in the last twelve months    21%
Others: I have stopped smoking and reduced drinking and started eating to compensate    6%

**8. *Sleep patterns***
Sound    64%
Restless    31%
Both    5%

**9. *Talking about your work to friends outside your school***
Enjoy it    48%
Obsessive/frequently complain about    24%
Don't talk about it    20%
Others: Both; normal amount of teacher talk and gentle moaning 8%

**10. Your health**
Good    67%
Symptoms not usually experienced
Irritable bowel (2); tearful and tired (1); stomach (1); skin problems
(1); headaches (1); heart palpitations (1)    33%

From the survey we learnt that our sample of teachers appeared to have
fewer symptoms of distress and anxiety than media hype led us to
expect. We also found that many had causes for anticipation and
delight. This is not to minimize the 'stress' so often perceived in teaching. We are trying instead to show that not all is doom and gloom.

## How are you coping with your distress, anxiety, anticipation and delight?

Answer the questions below to find out. The figures are the answers
from our research sample so you can compare yourself with them
immediately.

**11. How many hours per week do you estimate you work during
term time?**
| | |
|---|---|
| 0–35 | 1% |
| 35–39 | 5% |
| 40–44 | 17% |
| 45–49 | 10% |
| 50+ | 67% |

**12. How many weeks per year do you estimate that you spend
during school holiday periods without undertaking any lesson
preparation or administration/management for work activities?
(do not include in this any time spent 'reflecting' on work)**
| | |
|---|---|
| less than 1 | 2% |
| 1 | |
| 2 | 22% |
| 3 | 14% |
| 4 | 24% |
| 5+ | 36% |
| Not applicable | 2% |

**13. Do you consider that you have had situations in your personal life during the last three years with which you have had difficulty coping or which have caused you to feel seriously distressed?**

| | |
|---|---|
| Yes | 60% |
| No | 31% |
| Not answered | 9% |

**14. With which of these challenges have you had to cope during the past three years at work?**

| | No. of people in sample of 42 experiencing this factor | Percentage of sample experiencing each factor |
|---|---|---|
| Incompetent/difficult subordinates | 35 | 83 |
| Individual pupils with major social/psychological/learning difficulties | 34 | 80 |
| Particular class or year groups which were difficult to teach | 29 | 69 |
| Very demanding/difficult parents of pupils at your school | 29 | 69 |
| Inspection | 28 | 67 |
| Classes of more than 25 pupils | 27 | 64 |
| Unrealistic deadlines | 24 | 57 |
| Activities for which you were not trained | 20 | 48 |
| Financial difficulties | 18 | 42 |
| Activities you felt were beyond the responsibilities for which you were paid | 17 | 40 |
| Failure to gain a desired promotion/ new post | 15 | 36 |

| | | |
|---|---|---|
| Serious conflict with colleagues or governors | 15 | 36 |
| A bullying boss | 11 | 26 |
| Activities you felt were beyond your competence | 8 | 19 |
| No response | 2 | 5 |

This appears to be little different from the challenges facing recently qualified teachers. For these, anxiety and distress were short term and arose from individual teacher–pupil interactions with 'difficult' pupils, mixed ability teaching and whole-class disruption.

Some of our respondents listed other distressing or anxiety-inducing factors. These included job insecurity through being on fixed-term contracts, taking on new posts, supporting supply teachers, lack of support from local authorities and social service agencies, too much marking and poor accommodation.

**15. How much sick leave have you taken in the last three years which you consider was caused by you feeling unable to cope with factors such as those listed in Q.14?**
Seventy-nine per cent of our sample had taken no sick leave for any reason. The remainder did not consider that their illnesses had been related to anxiety or to distress.

**16a. What is (are) your principal leisure activities (i.e. not related to work or family responsibilities)?**
**16b. How much time per week do you estimate you spend on leisure activities?**

| Research sample grouped by numbers of leisure interests | Number of respondents | % of total sample | Average time on leisure | % of respondents in each leisure group working 50+ hours per week | % of respondents in each leisure group who are not senior managers |
|---|---|---|---|---|---|
| None | 3 | 7% | None | 100% | 66% |
| One | 6 | 14% | 6hrs, 40mins | 50% | 50% |
| Several | 31 | 74% | 11hrs, 12mins | 68% | 61% |
| No response | 2 | 5% | no response | | |

The few comments on this question demonstrated extreme contrasts from 'I have nothing like enough' or 'None at all', to 'I do 5–6 hours per week fitness class plus I have all my weekends for leisure'. There appeared to be little relationship between hours spent working and hours spent on leisure. Of those who worked the longest hours, some also played for long hours while others claimed to have little leisure time. Nor did leisure time appear to alter greatly if the respondents were senior rather than middle managers.

The range of leisure activities of the sample is an interesting indicator of teachers' interests. Any of them can

- give you at least temporary respite from distress;
- reduce or remove anxieties;
- offer pleasurable anticipation;
- provide the delight of success.

Do they accord with your interests? (The numbers in brackets are those in the sample who listed each leisure pursuit.)

*Arts*
Film (2); singing (1); photography (1); theatre (4).

*The social set*
Socializing (4); eating out (4); pub (2).

*Out and about*
Aircraft spotting (1); birdwatching (1); charity/church work (2); sunbathing (1); travel/holidays (6); window shopping (1).

*Sports*
Cricket (1); cycling and motor-cycling (4); football (2); keep-fit (4); general (3); gym (1); hockey (1); sailing (2); skiing (1); swimming (6); tennis (3); volleyball (1); walking (11); watching ice hockey (1); water-skiing (1); weight training (1); yoga (1).

*Home focus*
Cookery (1); construction (1); gardening (9); internet (1); listening to music (1); reading (8); studying (2); television (5).

## Helping yourself to cope with distress, anxiety, anticipation, delight

### Get the mind-set right

ALWAYS tell yourself you can cope, and REWARD yourself when you do.

DON'T expect too much of yourself. You cannot simultaneously be the perfect teacher, and school manager as well as, for example, an outstanding partner, parent, child, home decorator, sportsperson, singer and socialite. You will achieve all of these at some time in your life, but you'll need to select one at a time as your priority.

ACCEPT that you won't always succeed, but realize that neither does anyone else.

DISTRESS, ANXIETY, ANTICIPATION AND DELIGHT all help you to diet, to cope with pain and to think more efficiently! Our physical responses to these four states include moving the blood usually used for digestion to our muscles and lungs; our saliva production decreases and our mouths dry – all these discourage eating. Meanwhile, we release endorphins which reduce sensitivity to bruising (and possibly to bruised feelings). Extra hormones sharpen the brain to think of how to deal with problems.

TELL YOURSELF that you have coped before and you will do so again.

ASK YOURSELF what is the worst failure you can imagine; it's usually not that bad, so give it a go.

BE PLEASED when you successfully complete a task that was worrying you.

### Select strategies that offset distress and anxiety with anticipation and delight

#### Personal strategies

- Keep either Saturday or Sunday completely free of school issues.
- Cat-nap.
- Stroke the cat, dog, partner, children, your inside forearm.
- Plan something you look forward to, whether that is a weekend meal out or pot-holing.
- Undertake exercise that requires both mental concentration and physical activity.

- Trust yourself and be optimistic. This simple advice was published as long ago as 1964 (Caplan) but it is still very valid.
- Eat dark chocolate.
- Bake a cake, make models, paint – anything you can finish in a short time.
- Write down all the things you have achieved in a day.
- Praise yourself for what you have achieved rather than remembering what has not been done.

*Personal work strategies*

- Think positively. Isn't it great to have such a varied job that so immediately improves the achievements of others?
- When faced with an overwhelming pile of 'to do' items, select first something you *want* to do, not necessarily the most urgent or important as demanded by others.
- Set a limit to the amount of time you will devote to an activity.
- Break at lunchtime, read some real rubbish, go for a walk.
- Freely express your emotions – both positive and negative.
- Don't expect too much of yourself; if, for example, you targeted yourself to finish writing reports by late afternoon and you had to leave it to be completed the following morning, was this really failure? You have achieved a degree of success and can anticipate the pleasure of completion the following day.
- Pretend enthusiasm even if you don't feel it; you'll find it will convert to the real thing.

*Classroom and colleague organizational strategies*

- Classroom assistants could mark work and only refer to the teacher those pupils whose work indicates that they need particular guidance. In secondary schools, some self-marking, or group marking, could be organized.
- Use classroom assistants, or older pupils, to help young ones with, for example, clothing at the beginning and end of each day so you do not have to do it.
- Seek information to understand what is happening to you.
- Ask others for help.

- Break problems into manageable sections and deal with one at a time.
- Pace yourself – decide what is achievable in the time available and then add a little bit more in order to challenge yourself.
- *For high risk takers: suggest to your head of department, curriculum co-ordinator or headteacher that meetings might be cancelled for one week/term/year. If your idea is accepted, reflect on what happened, or did not happen, as a result. Can written memos or e-mails substitute for meetings? Alternatively, suggest a change in the times for meetings so they are not after school but held one morning per week only before school starts.*

## Helping your colleagues to cope with distress, anxiety, anticipation, delight

### Get the mind-set right

PRAISE your colleagues (superiors and subordinates) for their achievements. This includes praise for those who cope with anxiety and distress. Sincere, brief remarks and gestures can be done both individually and in group meetings. This is important because teachers spend their time largely with children from whom they get various types of feedback, but they need praise from other adults.

ENCOURAGE colleagues to share their emotions; join in their happiness or provide a shoulder to cry on. Such sessions release tensions.

HUMOUR helps. Everyone has to take the demands of school seriously, but feeling able to joke about league tables, action plans, etc., without fear of criticism for being light-hearted, is important.

### Select strategies that offset distress and anxiety with anticipation and delight

Distress and anxiety can arise when you and/or colleagues are expected to take on new tasks or alter established routines. How can you help colleagues to convert that to, at least, anticipation? Consider these examples:

- Your school has always had termly boarders, now there is demand to be met from pupils needing occasional overnight accommodation, so the head of boarding has to be more flexible.

- The school front office is to be redesigned so that it looks more welcoming to parents, but the new, open-plan situation makes the reception staff feel exposed.
- Classroom display is the job of the teaching assistant but you are worried that he won't do it as well as you can.
- Your school successfully applies to be allowed to set aside some of the National Curriculum and to devise its own subject plans. You have never produced your own curriculum before.
- Two new pupils join one of your classes – one pupil is seriously learning-impaired and the other has limited vision.

These are just a few of the types of changes with which school staff must cope. Each of them can be seen as an opportunity for anticipation and delight, but the initial reaction is more likely to be a groan at the extra work needed. The challenge is to prevent the groan becoming a long-drawn-out sigh. For this, try some of these suggestions.

*1. Understand why you/your colleagues are feeling distressed*
Their attitudes will be one of these.

- 'It's new – I could gain or lose work, money, status, authority.'
- 'I am afraid I don't have the skills to adapt to it.'
- 'I don't know how to deal with it – people might laugh at my failure.'
- 'I'm cross because it's been imposed on us and no one asked me if I wanted it.'
- 'It's just another change in endless change.'

When you are aware of which of these feelings is dominant, if you are in school leadership, you can devise strategies to eliminate them as far as possible and/or provide emotional support; if you are a colleague, or subordinate, show that you empathize or sympathize with colleagues. Consider if there are ways in which you can offer practical assistance.

## 2. Involve the activists first

Every management text will repeat the mantra that the more every-one has participated in a change and its planning, the more delighted will the whole school be about it. We haven't, however, yet found a management text that speaks of the likely anxiety from 'democratic fatigue' or the attitude that, 'You take the decisions, just let me get on with my job – I don't want any more meetings'. So, don't try to involve everyone. What is more important and effective in helping colleagues feel pleased about change is to involve, first, the doers – not the doubters. Pick the enthusiastic types first.

## 3. Ensure everyone knows why a change has to happen

Spread information. Give time for people to talk through anxieties and frustrations. Set up e-mail chat lines and keep updating on progress.

## 4. Market the delights of change

Be enthusiastic – it's catching. Advertise how the change will benefit yourself and others.

## 5. Provide tools, time and training for change

## 6. Establish a 'one-at-a-time' achievement culture

Decide on the change priority. Work on that one and finish it. With limited resources, you can't work successfully on all issues at once.

## 7. Value risk-taking

Be receptive to new ideas and initiatives. Offer opportunities to discuss them, even if it isn't possible to always go forward with them.

---

**STRESS MANAGEMENT TIP 2**

Welcome distress, anxiety, anticipation, delight as naturally created mental workouts. It's equivalent to going to a gym to create a physical workout artificially.

*Part Five*

# Success with Your Career

# 10 Your career in schools

*Angela Thody*

Start by checking out your career management to date. Have you followed the pattern below (or are you planning to)?

- *Year 1:* becoming known in your school; making others aware of your presence; enjoying the learning opportunities; enthusiastically participating in project management, e.g. school play, field trips.
- *Year 2:* first within-own-school promotion applications (primary or secondary); extending your range of project management opportunities to develop your career portfolio; beginning to attend short courses outside your own school. Those with aptitude and interest can fast track from here into management roles.
- *Years 3 and 4:* first promotions achieved/applications outside your own school; professional development through a planned programme of regular short courses; becoming an active member of your subject or professional association.
- *Year 5:* decision time.

Beyond Year 5, which is the route to follow? To decide this, consider the career portfolio you want to build.

## Building your career portfolio

Careers used to be seen only as linear. You went straight upwards from classroom teacher to headteacher, and any deviation was not well regarded. Now there is a wider view. What you are trying to build is a portfolio of experiences. It's still true that it may enhance your promotion chances if these experiences are grouped around a major 'line of interest', but moving across 'lines' shows the width of your abilities. These are likely to be prized since schools have had to become more responsive to their communities and to pupils' needs for wider preparation for the changing work and leisure markets of their futures.

---

*Your career portfolio – which line(s) do you most want to follow?*

⇨ *Management:* subject leadership; student welfare; middle management to senior leadership.

⇨ *Leader of other teachers' learning:* advanced skills' teacher; professional development tutor; teaching on courses organized by your local education authority or local university.

⇨ *Career break for family developments:* involvement in children's activities as, for example, playgroup/sports leader; upgrading your qualifications; participating in elderly relatives' activities; giving adult education and management experience, e.g. in charity/voluntary societies; school governorship or board membership; self-employed tutoring; school inspections; examining and marking.

⇨ *Alternative teaching:* special needs; teaching abroad; moving from the independent sector to the maintained sector or *vice versa.*

⇨ *Union representation:* usually voluntary and within your own school initially. You may then choose to move to regional or national level. Union representation, even at school level, rarely combines with promotion in other spheres concurrently.

⇨ *International experience:* short term (up to one year), e.g. for Europe, use the Central Bureau, for the Commonwealth, use the League of Commonwealth Teachers (addresses of these and other organizations are in this book's reference section); for all areas of the world, contact The British Council or The English Speaking Union. Longer term, e.g. teaching English as a foreign language, contracts with overseas development departments of government ministries, voluntary service overseas, permanent employment with international, and independent schools or with Service Children's schools – see the education press. Check before you go – will your school hold your job for you? Can you have it back at the same rate of pay and conditions as you have now? Are your teaching qualifications accepted in your intended destination (most do accept British qualifications but you will need to arrange registration by their teaching councils)?

Once you have selected your line(s), the next stage is to assess your abilities to get to where you want to go.

## Which of your abilities make your promotion most likely?

From the list in Figure 10.1 below, select the four characteristics which you think are most likely and least likely to gain you promotion in your own or other schools.

| Characteristics | Your top and bottom four |
|---|---|
| Administrative/managerial ability | |
| Personal/social contacts with those who can influence promotion | |
| Knowledge of government policies | |
| Subject expertise | |
| Flexibility/variety in teaching methods | |
| Strong personality | |
| Good relationships with staff | |
| Willingness to co-operate to meet with external inspection requirements such as OFSTED, | |
| Good appraisals | |
| Experience in a variety of schools/colleges | |
| Length of service | |
| Concern for pupils' welfare | |
| Holding/studying for a specialist qualification, e.g. for leadership or for special needs | |
| Ability to control pupils | |
| Conformity with/support for views of the school/college hierarchy | |
| Good relations with the headteacher and other senior staff | |
| Good relations with governors | |
| Leadership attributes | |
| Participation in extra-curricular activities | |
| Being innovative | |
| Pupils achieving good examination results | |
| Being in a shortage subject area | |
| Others – please specify | |

**Figure 10.1** Assessing your abilities for promotion

Now compare your answers with those below which I obtained from a small pilot survey in 1999. I asked senior school managers their views on which of the above characteristics most influenced their choices of which staff to promote, either from existing staff or from outside applicants.

### Getting promoted: adopt the right attributes
*Most important*
- leadership attributes;
- being innovative;
- exhibiting administrative and managerial abilities;
- having subject expertise.

*Rated as second most important attributes*
- concern for student welfare;
- strong personality;
- studying for higher degrees or specialist qualifications;
- participation in extra-curricular activities;
- flexible teaching methods;
- pupils getting good examination results.

*Least important*
- personal/social contacts with those who could influence promotion;
- knowledge of government policies;
- good relations with governors;
- being in a shortage subject area.

The group whom we consulted consisted of those most influential in school promotions (eleven headteachers from secondary schools; six headteachers from primary schools; two headteachers from special schools; one headteacher, a deputy headteacher and a house-master from independent schools; and six others – deputy headteachers, department heads, subject leaders). All had significant years of experience, including making staff appointments.

The sample was not large enough to work out if there were significant relationships between respondents' views and their types of schools, but the views did not vary greatly whatever the schools or colleges concerned.

- Primary, secondary and special school headteachers were equally likely to rate subject knowledge and studying for higher degrees as important.
- Primary headteachers rated concern for pupils' welfare slightly more highly than did secondary headteachers.
- Secondary headteachers rated abilities to control pupils, and to produce pupils with good examination results slightly more highly than primary headteachers.

Survey respondents were asked to suggest further characteristics which they thought important to promotion chances. Their additions were: (a) luck, (b) good timing, (c) excellent teaching, (d) influence in the staffroom and (e) knowledge of how pupils learn. How significantly would you rate these?

For readers aiming to become headteachers, it is worth considering the added attributes deemed vital for those wanting top posts. Headteachers should be:

- visionary;
- good communicators, approachable, ready to listen;
- fair, instilling discipline, concerned to achieve equity;
- motivators for staff;
- up to date with government policies;
- primarily committed to internal school matters, with low priority accorded to a role in the local or national communities. (Moos *et al.*, 1998)

## Which routes make your promotion most likely?

We reviewed the career paths of the 28 senior school staff in the above survey, with the following results.

### For promotions in primary schools

- Go for first promotion within three to four years of starting teaching.
- Expect to traverse three/four posts, over an average of twelve years, in more than one school, before becoming a headteacher.
- Travel via subject leadership to deputy headship in small schools, then move to larger schools.

### For promotions in secondary schools
- Go for first promotion within two years of starting teaching.
- Expect to traverse six posts, over an average of eleven years, before becoming headteacher.
- Travel via head of subject department (in a small department or small school) to head of a subject department (in a large department or large school) to head of faculty or sixth form to deputy headteacher.

### For promotions in independent schools
- Go for first promotion within four years of starting teaching.
- Expect to traverse six posts, over an average of 25 years.
- Travel via head of subject department to head of a house to deputy headteacher.

The general message is that if you want to get promoted quickly, it is better to follow a subject-based route, moving through schools or departments of increasing size. These findings are consistent with a 1993 review of research on this topic (Thody, 1993). Perhaps surprisingly, the findings are little changed from as long ago as 1974 (Hilsum and Start) and also accord with career patterns of Australian teachers (Maclean, 1992). There should, however, be changes in the 2000s worldwide because of demographic changes. Too few people are entering the teaching profession to fill the vacancies; many are due to retire within five-ten years; applications for headships are declining. The result of these are increased opportunities to fast track your career. The British government is advising school senior managers to select likely candidates for rapid promotions and special training in order to fill the forthcoming vacancies at senior levels.

This may mean that you will progress quickly even if you have a 'non-standard' background, unlike those in our late 1990s survey. Those few of our mini-survey group who took slightly longer than the rest to reach senior posts had non-standard career experiences. These included two or three years as local education authority advisory teachers or in school posts carrying pastoral rather than subject responsibilities; two had had career breaks for family reasons and had restarted their careers from the bottom again after the breaks (as did one of the authors of this book); one had become headteacher of two schools overseas in early career but had not then attained the same position on return to the home country. Those in special education had posts in mainstream schools first and varied experiences in different types of special education.

There was one factor our sample did not need to take into account in their past career movements but which you do need to consider. Do you move only to schools/colleges which are high in the league tables? From the early 1990s, all schools in England and Wales have been given a position in national league tables based on their examination results; some other countries are adopting similar systems.

Schools which are low in the league tables, or which are deemed to be 'failing' and/or have been placed in 'special measures' with the threat of possible closure, find it hard to attract staff. Thus your chances of getting the post you want in such schools are higher than in the successful schools which will pull in many more applications. It's possible, however, that it may be difficult to move on from low-rated schools.

Our advice would be to go for the lower-rated school if

1. it has a lively, determined and supportive headteacher and governors with clear policies likely to achieve improvements;
2. you don't intend to stay more than three years in that post (start applying for alternatives after two years);
3. the school roll is rising;
4. you feel you can help make a difference and that you will be credited with your achievements;
5. you want to work there;
6. the school's value added rating is good even if its examination results are not;
7. you're applying for the headship.

## Which characteristics make your promotion more difficult?

There is anecdotal, official and research evidence that it takes longer to get promoted if you are female, or non-white, or have a large number of children, or have no children, or are over 45, or are considered fat, ugly or unusually short, or have non-heterosexual tendencies or too many heterosexual tendencies, or qualifications in

PE, or extreme political views, or parents who were not teachers or . . .

The bad news is that this list seems to include anyone who is not white, male, of European origin and in a long-term partnership with 2.4 children. The good news is that a great many teachers don't fit this pattern, so you're not alone.

The good news is also that equal opportunities legislation, changing societal attitudes and teacher shortages have alleviated the worst excesses of rejection for factors unrelated to job performance. In the 2000s, there are so few applicants for management posts that it is becoming much easier to gain promotion early in your career. The bad news is that these developments have also been blamed for contrary effects; for example, since it became legally and societally allowed for men to be headteachers of girls' schools, the number of female headteachers has declined. Another example is the extension of parental leave which could militate against employing those likely to have responsibilities for their own children.

So, what should we do about the inequities that are likely to inhibit promotion unfairly? Most of them are factors we can't change (such as our sex) or can only marginally alter (such as our weight). Most of them are factors that will subconsciously influence those who select teachers for promotion, though all will try not to be prejudiced. We all tend to select as our friends/partners those who look and sound much like ourselves, the same tends to apply when we are making staff appointments.

In response to this, we have three choices. Which is yours?

1. Moan about the unfairness of life. Refuse to apply for promotion because 'I'll never get it because of my . . .'.
2. Be determined that people must accept you for what you are. Turn up for the interview in a droopy skirt with a mismatched top, bright green hair, a ring through the end of your nose and tell the panel you favour pupil selection by ability (your interview is in a non-streamed, non-selective comprehensive school).
3. Adapt to the prevailing culture. Schools as organizations need conformists with a spirit of individualism. So wear that suit but with a bright, ethnic shirt. Demonstrate you can help pupils achieve good examination results but that you

also have bright ideas for getting your politics pupils to act out a mock-legislature or for the incorporation of artistic creativity into primary numeracy.

Whether you chose (2) or (3), you can increase your chances by gaining qualifications.

## Which qualifications make your promotion most likely?

### Personal
#### University opportunities
Post-graduate certificates, diplomas and degrees, i.e. Masters, a professional doctorate (EdD) or a research doctorate (PhD). Distance learning and part-time degrees are now commonly offered so it is possible to combine work and studying.

#### Which course?
If you are still in your early years of teaching, then opt for subject enhancement or teaching skills improvement (e.g. Masters degrees in Chemistry or in Learning and Development). Beyond your first promotion or after five years, consider management qualifications, e.g. MBA, EdD in Educational Leadership.

#### Guidance and finance
Use your appraisal interview to discuss possibilities. Your school may be willing to fund courses related to the school's needs. Hence, find out school priorities from the development plan and ask to attend courses that will help the school with its objectives. Most university courses expect you to produce assignments related to your school's needs, so you can offer your school your services as a 'consultant'. Accept that you may have to pay for your own qualifications since you are improving your chances of moving on from your original school; banks offer career loans and most university fees for a three-year part-time graduate degree are less than the cost of one annual holiday.

### Government
Government-financed qualification opportunities change frequently according to political priorities, so watch the education press and

your staffroom noticeboard. Government funding will cover fees, and sometimes the money also provides for substitute staff to cover your absence on courses. Universities may recognize some courses as providing exemption from parts of Masters degrees.

*Examples (England and Wales)*
*Management training:* this list demonstrates the variety offered in the past 30 years; watch for changing opportunities in the next 30!

- 2003 onwards: headship induction programmes, training programmes for middle management
- 2001/2: National College for School Leadership for aspiring and serving headteachers
- 1998: national professional qualifications for aspiring and serving headteachers
- 1996: headlamp for newly appointed headteachers
- 1992: mentoring for newly appointed headteachers
- 1980s: diplomas and degrees on full-time secondment for aspiring headteachers, senior and middle managers
- 1970s: one-term training opportunities for headteachers and for departmental leaders

*Shortage subject training:* bursaries have been offered for basic training in, for example, technology, modern languages, mathematics. Advanced skills in these, and other areas, may attract government funding.

*Research funds:* grants from 1998 to help teachers to conduct and publish their own classroom research.

*Fast track teacher:* for graduates willing to work extra hours for more rapid promotion.

*Advanced skills teachers*: for those wanting promotion but not into management. The posts entail 20 per cent release from classroom teaching in order to help provide induction, mentoring and training of newly qualified teachers, guiding and providing professional development for other teachers.

### School opportunities for qualifications
*Professional development days*
Participate actively, offer to be a presenter.

*In-school accredited courses*

Schools now negotiate with local universities for courses provided by the school to be accredited as part of higher degrees or for teachers to gain credit for particular types of project management. Does your school offer this?

*School staff development policy*

Does your school hold an Investors In People award, or similar? If so, they are committed to training you and it may be easier for you to obtain financial support for courses outside the school. Find out what is your school's staff development policy, how it awards finance and leave to attend courses and what courses other staff are attending. Get to know who holds the staff development budget; make them aware of your interest in self-improvement; be helpful to them in other ways.

## Organization opportunities for qualifications

*Unions, professional associations, local authority, school board, organizations of special schools, independent schools or faith schools, conference centres.*

All offer numerous short courses, some of which are accredited to qualification through a university.

Advantages:

- spreading your networking so you meet those from other schools and areas who can help guide your promotion;
- courses tend to relate to the most recent developments since these organizations can most quickly adapt what they offer to current needs;
- provide tasters so you can assess the direction you wish your career to take;
- require only short periods out of school and no long-term commitment.

---

**CAREER MANAGEMENT TIP 1**

- Create a portfolio of both accredited and non-accredited courses and of short and long courses.
- Select courses linked around only one or two career lines.
- Keep records of all courses attended – topics and outcomes – even for one-day courses.

---

## Career planning?

All the commentary so far assumes that you are making career plans. Studies of promoted teachers indicate that most did have career plans (though at least one of the authors of this book did not but still got promoted!). Studies of career decision-making, however, show uncertainty about the extent to which you can direct your own career planning, or how far your choices are determined by circumstances, or are a mixture of both your choices and your situation (Hodgkinson, 1998, p. 558).

We would advise adopting whichever approach best suits your personality and your circumstances. Drifters and risk-takers won't plan; the organized and risk-averse will plan; those who have to live in particular areas for family reasons will have plans made for them. Whichever way you follow, you need a mind-set that you *want* promotion.

## Enhancing your promotion chances

Well, I don't really know. My degree result wasn't as good as hoped, but I could have gone on for retail management if I'd really wanted, but I thought well – teaching – why not? (Student teacher, overheard in a school staffroom, responding to the question, 'What made you want to teach?')

This potential teacher presumably did not envisage a teaching career, otherwise the comments would have followed our second tip:

---

**CAREER MANAGEMENT TIP 2**

Sound, and look, positive about yourself, others and your school/college.

---

The rationale for this tip lies in recognizing that career management is not a once-a-year planning operation but is ongoing. Your attitudes, achievements and behaviours are being constantly (though usually subconsciously) evaluated by those colleagues who can influence your promotion prospects.

You may be lucky enough to have a formal, and/or informal, mentor who is guiding your career. If so, take your mentor's advice and cultivate the contact. It is interesting to note that in our 1999 mini-survey on career progress reported earlier in this chapter, the group did not rate highly this nurturing of contacts, whereas in the Hilsum and Start 1974 survey, it featured significantly. Personal experience leads us to favour the older view.

Meanwhile, the rest is up to you. You are the only one who knows all that you have achieved, who has a vested interest in ensuring that it is known, and who will put it in the best light possible.

---

**CAREER MANAGEMENT TIP 3**

Career management needs

- persistence (you are always selling yourself);
- personality (you are your main sales agent);
- presentation skills (you use these to demonstrate your abilities).

---

## Keeping career records

KEEP AN ACCOUNT OF *EVERYTHING* YOU HAVE DONE. Add activities to your CV as you do them. Then you have all the information ready for job applications. You won't have to dredge around in your memory for the date you led the working party on relations with support staff or for the years you taught Year 1 before moving to Year 3.

SELECT FROM YOUR FULL CV THE ITEMS IMPORTANT TO THE JOB FOR WHICH YOU ARE APPLYING. Demonstrate how your experience and abilities match what a particular school or college requests. Hence if a job description for a subject leader requires ability to demonstrate knowledge of Key Stage 2 requirements, then the first item in your supporting letter will stress that you have been teaching Year 6 and attending a training course for Key Stage 2. If the first request by the advertisers highlights the appointing school's need for good team workers, your supporting letter will begin with how the team in your department operates or how you participated in the team planning the school's centenary celebrations.

MIND THE GAPS. As you watch your career records grow, aim to achieve the most comprehensive experiences possible, especially if you want a headship. In primary schools, for example, try to teach all the Key Stages; in secondary schools, look for both pastoral and curriculum responsibilities.

If you don't already have career records, then start them now. Preferably, maintain them on a word processor for ease of updating, but file cards will do as well. If using the latter, keep one for each entry within each of the four areas below.

### Your career – what to record
*Basics*
- address, phone, fax, e-mail;
- teacher's registration number;
- National Insurance number;
- date of birth;
- your schools with dates of attendance;
- qualifications – start with the highest level and most recent first, unless requested otherwise, i.e. degree(s), teacher training, A levels, GCSE; others such as first aid, life saving, health and safety, languages, etc. (all with dates and grades, awarding organization – you will find it astonishing that many years after completing your own school education, you are still required to provide details of it);
- referees – addresses, phone, fax, e-mail – so you can contact them quickly when a job application is imminent; you must

get their agreement to act as a referee and preferably send them a copy of your application;

- personal interests – few schools request information about these now (perhaps they recognize that few teachers have time to continue with their personal interests!) but keep a record, especially if hobbies are relevant to school/college, e.g. you play a trumpet in a brass band.

## Posts to date

Maintain this list in reverse chronological order and unless an application form instructs otherwise, present the information in that order. For each of your jobs, record

- school/college, employing organization;
- dates you were employed – make sure there are no unexplained gaps. If you were unemployed for a period, explain what you did, e.g. family career break, travel abroad;
- title of your posts, salary scale and salary;
- brief description of the main responsibilities you held in each post;
- part-time employment related to teaching, e.g. examination marking, private tutoring, leading adult education classes.

## Professional development

This is all the formal and informal learning activities undertaken since your first appointment.

- all topics of in-house staff development days;
- short courses attended, topics, dates;
- qualifications in progress – keep a list of the subjects studied, titles of your dissertations and assignments. Any of these gives you a claim to expertise in an area that you may not have from your experience but will have from your studies;
- experience of mentoring or being mentored;
- membership of professional associations and examples of any involvement such as committee work or attending conferences;
- publications – you can make a start on these through writing

for your teachers' newsletter for your area, or for the magazines of your professional association;

- voluntary/community activities, especially where related to teaching, e.g. being a school governor, running a youth club, or which demonstrate managerial competences, e.g treasurer for the senior citizens' lunch club, secretary for the pub quiz league;
- travel: include only travel for professional reasons (*not* holidays – but you can mention gap year experiences if you are relatively new to teaching).

*Competences/experience*

- teaching – subjects and ages, examinations for which you have prepared candidates, examination results of your classes, teaching methods used and developed;
- subject management, e.g. development work;
- financial/resources management, e.g. a budget for which you are responsible;
- people management, e.g. have you had to deploy classroom assistants, laboratory technicians or parents as helpers? Do you work in a team? What is your part in the team?
- marketing/public relations management, e.g. working on a committee designing the school prospectus; meetings with parents; visiting feeder schools to encourage pupils to enrol at your school;
- community relations, e.g. your personal involvement in local groups; do you take your pupils to meet people in residential homes? Have you incorporated local people into your environment development programme?

---

### CAREER MANAGEMENT TIP 4

*Never* send the same CV or supporting letter for different promotion applications. Adjust the focus, the prioritized details and how you stress your abilities to match the requirements of the job.

# 11 Education careers outside schools

*Angela Thody*

At what point do you become ready for career progression? Should you stay in teaching or move to allied professions? This chapter helps you with these decisions.

## Ready to move on?

In the following quiz (Figure 11.1):

- Score 1 for closest match to your current career.
- Score up to 5 to indicate distance away from your requirements.
- Score nil for questions you omit as unimportant, or not applicable, to you.
- The nearer your final score is to 215, the more you are ready to change your career.

(*Note:* in the questions, family = those living with you/dependent on you.)

*Circle your score*

SECURITY FOR SELF AND FAMILY

| | |
|---|---|
| Is the salary enough to meet your perceived personal and family needs? | 0...1...2...3...4...5 |
| Is your housing adequate, safe, pleasant? | 0...1...2...3...4...5 |
| Are there schools/colleges nearby suited to the needs of partners and other family members? | 0...1...2...3...4...5 |
| Are there medical and care facilities nearby suitable for family members? | 0...1...2...3...4...5 |
| Are there career opportunities nearby for other family members? | 0...1...2...3...4...5 |
| Are your personal and occupational environments physically and environmentally safe? | 0...1...2...3...4...5 |
| Do you feel that your pension scheme will provide adequately for your needs? | 0...1...2...3...4...5 |
| Are you on a permanent contract in your main teaching job? | 0...1...2...3...4...5 |

## SOCIABILITY

| | |
|---|---|
| Do you have strong ties/social links in the area? | 0...1...2...3...4...5 |
| Does your family have strong ties/social links in the area? | 0...1...2...3...4...5 |

Does your main teaching job offer you:

| | |
|---|---|
| the scope you need to express your individuality? | 0...1...2...3...4...5 |
| the amount of team working you enjoy? | 0...1...2...3...4...5 |
| the social contacts you want? | 0...1...2...3...4...5 |

If your teaching post does not provide you with the sociability that you want,

| | |
|---|---|
| is this adequately compensated for by family, hobbies, voluntary work? | 0...1...2...3...4...5 |

## PRESENT CAREER ENVIRONMENT

In your current teaching post:

| | |
|---|---|
| do the timetable and holiday arrangements meet personal and family needs? | 0...1...2...3...4...5 |
| is there adequate opportunity for your academic satisfaction? | 0...1...2...3...4...5 |
| are there enough professional development opportunities for you? | 0...1...2...3...4...5 |
| do you like your immediate boss? | 0...1...2...3...4...5 |
| do you respect your immediate boss? | 0...1...2...3...4...5 |
| do you have enough 'perks', e.g. car pool, free car parking, help with housing costs, car loans, medical insurance? | 0...1...2...3...4...5 |
| do you believe in what your school tries to do? | 0...1...2...3...4...5 |
| do you have satisfactory relationships with colleagues? | 0...1...2...3...4...5 |

If your teaching post does not provide you with the career environment that you want, is this adequately compensated for by family, hobbies, voluntary work?　0...1...2...3...4...5

## POLITICS

In your teaching post, do you have:

| | |
|---|---|
| the degree of involvement in decision-making that you want? | 0...1...2...3...4...5 |
| as much power/influence over budgets as you want? | 0...1...2...3...4...5 |
| as much power/influence over other staff as you want? | 0...1...2...3...4...5 |
| as much freedom to take decisions without referral to other staff as you want? | 0...1...2...3...4...5 |
| as much opportunity to be guided by other staff as you want? | 0...1...2...3...4...5 |

If your teaching post does not provide you with the political power/influence you want, is this adequately compensated for by activities in your family, hobbies, voluntary work?　0...1...2...3...4...5

Are your family satisfied with the politics of your teaching post and other activities?　0...1...2...3...4...5

STATUS

In your teaching post, do you feel that your abilities and contributions are

    recognized in:

| | |
|---|---|
| Your job title and grade? | 0...1...2...3...4...5 |
| Your salary? | 0...1...2...3...4...5 |
| Your office accommodation? | 0...1...2...3...4...5 |
| Your classroom accommodation? | 0...1...2...3...4...5 |
| Your parking space? | 0...1...2...3...4...5 |
| Your role at school and college public events? | 0...1...2...3...4...5 |
| Your rights to participate in extra professional events during school time? | 0...1...2...3...4...5 |
| the respect accorded to you by students, colleagues, parents, superiors, governors? | 0...1...2...3...4...5 |
| opportunities for career enhancement or development? | 0...1...2...3...4...5 |

Is there a satisfactory mechanism for evaluation of status through,

    e.g., appraisal, performance-related pay?     0...1...2...3...4...5

If your teaching post does not provide you with the status you want, is this

    adequately compensated for by family, hobbies, voluntary work?     0...1...2...3...4...5

Are your family satisfied with your status in your teaching post and other

    activities?     0...1...2...3...4...5

Are you now as well qualified as your immediate superior?     0...1...2...3...4...5

**TOTAL**

**Figure 11.1**  Assessing your readiness to change your career

## How to move on

Leaving an established career for a new line of business is no longer the preserve of the career-break parent or a sign of failure: it's in line with current trends in the labour market.

Jobs for life are a past idea even in a profession like teaching, thought previously to be so secure. It's not unusual to have several careers during your working life. If you're interested in moving through different careers after only a few years in teaching, this isn't peculiar: see it instead as consciously planning to use all your different abilities.

Even ageism is gradually being reduced as a hindrance to starting new careers. The USA has pioneered the removal of compulsory retirement ages for university teachers – how soon will that cross the Atlantic?

Your answers to the opening quiz indicated that you're ready for a move. Are you ready for a move right *now*?

## STEPS TO CAREER CHANGE

**Talk to your family**
If your career change is going to affect them, how do they feel about it? Their support will be helpful.

↓

**Reassess your qualifications**
Can they lead in a different direction? Are you still young enough to start a new career at the bottom? Can you cope with income reduction while training for higher rewards later? e.g. with a maths, stats or economics degree, how about becoming an actuary? (pay on entry in 2004, £17,500–£24,000; up to three years' experience, £37,000–£58,000).

↓

**Get the mind-set right**
You *can* do it. You *will* do it. It's *right* to do it.

↓

**Choose how to depart**
1. Leave without another job in prospect.
2. Wait until an alternative application is successful or your own business is operational.
3. Check whether anything is likely to change at your school that might persuade you to stay, e.g. a new head, school reclassification or merger, pay rise. If so, will this overcome your frustrations in your current job?

↓

**Clarify your main reason(s) for leaving**
Your new career *must* satisfy these. Do you want more money, greater job satisfaction, to meet personal/family needs or a new boss or organization?

↓

**Know the transferable skills you've acquired from teaching**
*Which of these are yours?*
making written and oral presentations
research, data analysis
managing and motivating groups
project planning, management and leadership
motivating colleagues
team working
financial management
IT support, advice, knowledge
coping with difficult customers
creativity
ability to work unsupervised

↓

**Learn how to sell yourself to new employers or to prospective business partners or funders**

Make your CV relevant and applicable to the job you want. Don't present it as a list of your teaching achievements.

Research the organization to which you are applying.

Use any networks you have.

Remember – it takes a seasoned interviewer no more than one to five minutes to decide if you are the candidate for the job. Dress appropriately, walk, talk, sound and sit positively. Plan your body language.

Look at others' business plans before presenting yours to the bank or other lender.

Pay for professional advice. Attend a business course.

↓

**Assess your abilities and interests**

*Career analysis* – through local or commercial careers advice services. List your personal and career history, your interests and attitudes, then do their aptitude tests. You will be interviewed on issues such as family and marital context, organization of work and home life, best and worst experiences of the past five years. There will be a detailed assessment of your strengths and weaknesses which can take a morning or several days. Expect to pay around £400 to £1,000 (2004 prices).

*Life coaching* – a personal, life-skills coach to support and guide your self-help. The coach focuses you on what you want and how to get it. You are encouraged to empower yourself. The coach analyses you and sets stretching but realistic goals for a time period. Expect to pay at least £15 per half-hour (2004 prices) for telephone coaching, more if it's face-to-face.

*Escape training* – a teacher sets up a course to help would-be escapees to reassess their lives, fantasize about their futures and evaluate leaving options. Look around for similar ones or start a business in one yourself.

**Figure 11.2**   Your steps to career change

# Where to move to

This chapter concerns careers outside teaching but still allied to education. Obviously, you could try any career, from nuclear scientist to pop star to refuse disposal operative or novelist depending on your qualifications, abilities, interests and networks. We're assuming that you are still interested in education, though not in mainstream teaching.

Start with the education press, easily accessible on the internet. In just one week in 2004, in Britain's main job sources, The *Guardian Education* and *The Times Education Supplement*, there were advertised posts which were either outside schools or were inside schools but did not involve teaching. These included:

- joint university/local authority post to research ways to encourage disaffected pupils to aim for higher education;
- assistant education officer to research and support personnel policy developments;
- teacher co-ordinator for a charity to support children with literacy challenges;
- assistant at an outdoor pursuits and community centre in London;
- children's activity day care managers for the summer vacation;
- teaching and learning manager for an education action zone;
- professional development assistant for a teachers' association;
- education officer to produce teaching materials for a zoo;
- manager in a school for systems support and e-learning;
- manager to help develop a healthy schools initiative;
- learning resource manager for a lifeboat charity;
- professional development adviser with the DfES;
- education officer for Elective Home Education;
- education training officer for a pet care facility;
- school finance or business managers/bursars;
- leaders for a world challenge adventure trip;
- temporary broadband development manager;
- manager to develop SEN outreach services;
- education leaders for military museums;
- ethnic minority achievements adviser;
- children's homework centre leader;
- English and literacy consultant;
- 14–19 development co-ordinator;
- consultant in primary strategy;
- recruitment strategy adviser;
- governor services officer;
- adventure centre leader;
- education social worker;
- E-learning co-ordinator;
- learning mentors.

There must be at least one of these you might try for – and each week produces different opportunities.

A recently developed school-related new career is that of the bursar, or business manager. Self-managing schools, which have been emerging worldwide since the mid-1980s, need managers who relieve teaching staff of the commercial side of the operation. The business managers have responsibility for staffing, budgets, grounds, resourcing, sites and marketing, amongst others. Some teachers are transferring to this career route. There are bursars' professional associations for both the independent and state sectors. National training standards and an accreditation framework were established in 1998/9 and there is an MBA for school bursars from which some are proceeding to PhDs and EdDs. The National College for School Leaders set up certificate and diploma courses for bursars in 2003. Business managers usually join their school's senior management teams and some are designated as deputy headteachers.

## Short-term covering for absent teachers

While you're making up your mind on whether to follow a new career or not, why not use the 'halfway house' of joining an agency, or getting on the local authority's list for supply, relief or substitute teachers? How to do this successfully is described in the next chapter and do remember that the market is a seller's one, especially since the 2003 British government regulations limiting the amount of cover for absent colleagues which permanent staff can do. Schools increasingly outsource their teachers when

- they need to cover maternity, sickness and parental leaves;
- budget deficits preclude employing full-time staff who need full holiday pay and employment benefits in addition to salary;
- shortage subject staff can't be replaced;
- rolls unexpectedly rise;
- there are more pupils interested in an examination subject than expected;
- a school is in an unpopular location (the largest number of vacancies and the highest pay is in the London area; some agencies target particular areas only);
- specialists are needed (there are now agencies focused solely on, for example, special needs, modern languages).

If you don't want to teach at all, why not launch a career as a manager in a supply agency or set up a new one in your own specialism or area? The jobs include placing teachers in long-term and short-term posts, liaising with schools concerning their vacancies, and interviewing applicants.

According to one advertisement for an agency manager, you'll need to be an independent self-starter, well organized, a team player, a good telephone communicator, flexible, friendly, empathetic, intuitive, diplomatic and, of course, 'in possession of a good sense of humour' (which seems to be a requirement of every education-allied job!).

## Possibilities for a portfolio career

While doing agency work, you can also set up your own business as a consultant. The part-time jobs then become part of your consultancy profile. Many who have left teaching have followed this route. They add to their portfolios with school inspection, running school development days, participating as tutors on the government's schemes for training and retraining headteachers, and management training for industry. There is a Society of Education Consultants in Britain which you can join. Advice, inspection, professional development and consultancy are provided by various companies, all of which need employees. They offer both full-time and part-time posts.

Education consultancy pays around £200 to £1,000 per day at 2004 prices but check that it includes preparation time. Better rates emerge in management consultancy or project consultancy. These are harder to break into without commercial experience, but it's not impossible.

Personal businesses don't necessarily have to involve you in teaching. Why not market your teaching resources? Most of us have cupboards full of them. They need professionalizing from your egg boxes and sugar paper, but there are companies ready to help with this. They particularly seek out teachers' ideas, and you get around 5 per cent of the royalties. It's not a fortune, but it can add to your business portfolio. You might also be the one teacher who invents the school equivalent of *Trivial Pursuit* (for the cynics reading this, we don't mean the National Curriculum!). One ex-teacher, Robert Ives, set up *The Flying Pig Company* selling easy-to-make paper animated models which are now sold world-wide.

Royalties also come from writing books (around 10 per cent of the purchase price) or articles for professional newspapers or journals (but don't expect more than around £100–£200 at 2004 prices). These have the bonus of making your name better known, and other consultancy jobs become easier to obtain.

Part-time tutoring outside of schools is another useful addition *en route* to your new career, or as part of your new portfolio career. Distance learning organizations need such staff. In addition to the long-established Open University, many other universities now offer similar courses, often to students abroad. Contact your local university to see what are the possibilities. There are numerous local and national commerical tutoring agencies for which you could work with school age children or you can set up your own personal individual tutoring service advertising in your local media. Some national providers franchise their teaching materials for such private tuition so you would not even have to produce your own tutoring materials.

Adult and further education offer you jobs in teaching everything from acrobatics to Zen. These you can develop from your personal leisure interests, but your teaching skills can be of direct use for courses in communications, languages, training classroom assistants, helping those with learning difficulties and in Adult Basic Education. Contact your local Governor Support Unit to see if you could teach school governors.

Examination invigilation is now on offer, since by 2005 all British schools must cease using their permanent teaching staff for invigilation. This offers an additional job route to the better-known setting and marking of examination papers (the latter is discussed in the next chapter).

## Will you jump or be pushed?

Are you or your school likely to become redundant? If so, will you go before, or after the inevitable?

Going afterwards gives you the certainty of a redundancy package and possibly free help from counselling or out-placement firms. Conversely, potential employers may see you as negative and reactive. Going before should give you a greater choice of jobs, and prospective employers should see you as enterprising and positive.

But it also depends on the reasons for the redundancy. If, for example, your school is being merged or its type is being changed, then there can be some enhanced or alternative job prospects worth waiting for. If it is closing because of declining standards or numbers, the sooner you move, the better.

## Is it easy to change careers?

No, but it isn't easy to stay in teaching if you don't like it. For your new career, you will initially, almost certainly

1. work longer hours than you did in teaching, though the timings will be more flexible;
2. earn less than you did in teaching (plus you'll need to cover your own welfare benefits);
3. veer widely from euphoria to terror;
4. have to go out and market yourself aggressively, network continuously, chase up every contact, get used to telling people how fantastic you are.

Once through those early stages, you'll then be able to assess if it's worth staying out of teaching. Your new career need not be permanent. It's possible to move in and out of teaching. Going back may be worthwhile if you've satisfied alternative ambitions, have not enjoyed the change or if there are new opportunities in teaching.

# 12  Supply teaching and examining

*Amber Lascelle*

## What next? What else?

> 'I need a new challenge!'
>
> 'Paperwork, admin, paperwork . . . there must be more to teaching than this.'
>
> 'I want to extend my experience wider into different fields, not higher into management.'
>
> 'I need more time to spend looking after my parents.'
>
> 'I want a little extra for that South of France holiday.'
>
> 'I'll never be able to pursue my writing/painting/acting career while I'm teaching full-time.'
>
> 'I want to move into a different school – but what if I make the leap and it's the wrong choice?'

You might find yourself one day staring out of a classroom window, thinking something like the statements you read above, and realizing you want to look outside the bounds of full-time classroom teaching for something that better suits how you want your lifestyle to be.

Teachers make changes in their careers for hundreds of different reasons: necessity, changed circumstances, desire for new opportunities. This chapter looks at two different brave new worlds: supply teaching and examining for national tests such as Standard Attainment Tests (SATs which all pupils in England and Wales take at ages 7, 11 and 13) and the General Certificate in Secondary Education (GCSEs which all pupils take at ages 15/16 in between five and ten subjects).

## Supply teaching

### *Leaving the world of full-time teaching*

There may be a catalyst: a blow-up with management, the last-straw trials of 11B, a sudden opportunity or obligation in another area of your life. There may be a slow evolution: a growing discomfort with the ethos of your department, the demands of your life outside of teaching becoming more important. Whatever the reason, you're looking for a change. Could supply teaching be for you? It's variously termed substitute, cover, replacement or relief teaching depending on where you live but it means taking a temporary post for anything from half a day to two terms.

### *Supply versus full-time: can you make the leap?*

Ask yourself:

- Can you cope with being thrown in at the deep end?
- Can you adapt quickly to different environments and ideologies?
- Can you deliver a lesson off the cuff with no materials or lesson plan, in the face of 32 restless 16-year-old boys, and still make it a meaningful learning experience?

If you can answer 'Yes' to the above, or if at least you think it sounds like an interesting challenge, then supply teaching could be for you. Supply teaching allows you to focus entirely on your classroom practice and dispense with planning, marking, reports and a lot of paperwork. It enables you to practise your craft of teaching rather than a subject specialism.

In supply teaching, you will meet very different challenges every day. If you are looking for full-time work, it gives you the opportunity to 'try out' different schools in your area and see which is right for you (it could also put you in a good position when a full-time post does come up, if you have already taught in the school). It gives you the autonomy to decide your own hours, since you can do as much or as little as you like (there is almost always plenty of supply teaching to go around, so finding work should be relatively easy). If you find a school that you like, you can become their number one choice for supply cover – and if you spend a day in one that you hate, you need never go back.

Supply teaching has its drawbacks, primarily issues of pay and security. A full-time post gives you a regular paycheque, paid holidays and sick leave, and your job is always there. With supply teaching, if you are ill, you can't earn money, and there's little work around during the school holidays. In addition, you lose the continuity that a full-time post gives you. You may be thrilled to be free of 11B and their truancy, swearing, lack of coursework and impossible behaviour, but you also lose lovely 8D, with whom you have forged a real rapport and who tell you that you're the best teacher they ever had.

It's well known that students will 'play-up' a supply teacher and try to get away with more than with their regular teacher: '. . . but Miss Taylor *always* lets us take our ties off/sit with whoever we like/climb out of the windows . . .', and you are at a disadvantage through being unfamiliar with a new school's systems and protocol. Supply teaching can be isolating, as you no longer have your own department, and it takes time to get to know new names and faces in the staffroom.

However, there are ways of surmounting all of these issues.

---

### SUPPLY TEACHING TIP 1

If you're going to do it, go for it! Chin up and smile: bags of confidence (even if slightly faked) will carry you through and make your supply teaching career enjoyable.

---

## Supply teaching practicalities – jobs and pay

### Finding a job

When you decide to begin supply teaching, you have a number of options. One is to sign up with a supply agency. The agency will find you work and administer your pay. Your contact will be with the agency and not a school itself, so if you have a problem there is always a buffer zone.

*Agency employment*

Expect an interview when you sign up, much like a full-time teaching job interview. The interviewer will ask what sort of work you seek: long-term cover, short-term, day-to-day, and how much notice you require – from a week in advance down to the morning of the day you are needed. Well-established agencies often offer a guaranteed income option: so long as you are prepared to go to any school when they require, you can be paid a retainer even on days on which the agency does not find you work (be aware, though, that if they offer only a morning's teaching, you will have to accept it). Most agencies pay after the first two weeks, and weekly thereafter, although some are now attached to Local Education Authorities (LEAs) and in these you will be paid monthly, like other LEA employees.

*LEA employment*

Alternatively, you can contact the LEA for your area yourself (your local telephone directory will have contact numbers). LEAs have supply teachers' registers which are circulated to schools in the area. The schools then contact you directly to arrange work. Your pay is administered by the council, to whom you submit a time sheet each month.

Application packs for supply teachers, for both agencies and LEAs, include a generic application form, occupational health check, bank and payment information and a Criminal Records Bureau (CRB) Enhanced Disclosure form. The LEA or agency will pay for your CRB check to be carried out. Warning: be aware that the CRB check can take several weeks to complete, and you will not be allowed to teach until it has been done.

**Make your own luck**

Once you are registered with the LEA, get moving. You are in a very strong position as a qualified, registered supply teacher who has had occupational health and police checks carried out recently. Ask the council for a list of schools, and if you have access, use the internet to help you decide which ones are right for you. Find school websites, or visit the Independent Schools Council Information Service (ISCis) for a list of private schools in your area. Pick perhaps six or seven schools, and send your CV with a covering letter.

- Briefly outline your specialisms and a little on your background and experience. Tailor it to the school: for example, if it is a specialist sports college, mention that you coached the Year 8 cricket team; if it's a high-achieving academic school, note that you created your last school's Gifted and Talented programme.
- Say you are registered and cleared with the LEA, who can be contacted for information.
- Say you are keen to come and visit the school and have a chat with the deputy head/principal/ whoever is in charge of supply cover.
- If you wish, mention that you visited the website and that what you saw (be specific) encouraged you to apply.
- Offer to take certificates: your degree, your teaching qualification, your CRB form, your QTS certificate.
- Give contact details, and 'look forward to hearing from them'.

It is highly likely that you will receive calls within a few days, much sooner that waiting for the LEA register to be updated and circulated. If you don't receive anything from your initial blitz, go back to the list of schools, find some more, and repeat the process. School supply co-ordinators could contact an agency or go to the LEA list, but if your name and letter are there in front of them, guess who's first in line for that phone call?

### Pay me . . . PLEASE!

Try to determine your level of pay before you even begin teaching. Notify the LEA of your point on the pay spine and send evidence if you can (a letter from your last LEA, for example). Finance departments can be excruciatingly slow to process supply teachers' pay, and you may end up being paid an NQT salary, or worse, 'minimum unqualified instructors' rate' for a couple of months before they rectify it.

Check out your hourly rate from the pay spine (your union should be able to help you). Remember, if you provide supply cover in a special school you should receive an extra hourly payment – so check your payslip closely.

With LEA supply teaching, you can opt to continue paying your teachers' pension contributions, or to stop them, whilst with agency teaching, you often don't get the choice to carry on paying.

---

### SUPPLY TEACHING TIP 2

Always check your payslip. Don't assume it is correct – check the number of days, hourly rate, extras such as National Insurance payments. You may need to make a few phone calls to the finance department to correct your wages!

---

## Finding out about the schools

The ball is in your court as a supply teacher. Schools need you, and it is up to you to find out as much information as you can about the school so that you know it is right for you.

---

### SUPPLY TEACHING TIP 3

Forewarned is forearmed: it's wise to visit first if you can, as you will have plenty to deal with on your first day just with teaching and getting around. Find out as much information as you can before you even start teaching.

---

When you visit the school, or on your first day: ask, Ask, ASK! Schools will be encouraged to see someone who clearly wants to become a part of the school and provide continuity in meaningful cover lessons, rather than being a glorified babysitter.

Things you need to find out are:

*The discipline and reward system*
For example, if they have merits or credit slips, make sure you get some and that you understand the system. Some schools have highly complex systems of colour-coding according to good behaviour, excellent work, trying hard, good citizenship, and so on. Find out if there are home-school diaries to write in. Discuss the discipline policy until you are satisfied that you will be able to deal with

classroom situations in the same way as other teachers at the school. Be wary of the phrase 'We don't have behaviour problems'. Life for a supply teacher is very different from that of a deputy head who commands silence simply by his presence in a room! When you actually come to teach, find out the name of the head of your department for that day. Threatening to report behaviour issues 'to Mr Simpson' is a lot more effective than 'to whoever the Head of Science is'!

### How to get around the school

This may be as simple as obtaining a map, but could also include door codes and one-way corridor systems.

### The process with registers and assemblies

Do you send the register back to the office with a student or bring it yourself? What time are assemblies? What time means 'late' on the register?

### The timetable

Don't find out *on Wednesday afternoon* that Year 11 leave early on that day even though it isn't on the regular timetable! Does the school have bells, buzzers, or nothing at all?

### The magic portals: keys and cupboards

Lesson time can be wasted, and behaviour worsen, as you cast about looking for textbooks and sending students to other teachers to chase up keys. Try to find out if you'll need to see the head of department to get access to books, paper and so on.

### Staffroom protocol

In some, you can buy tea and coffee from the kitchen staff or a vending machine; others offer the staffroom tea and ask for a few pence in the kitty; in others, you would be wise to bring your own flask (and a portable, folding chair to avoid taking someone else's seat)!

If you can't visit the school in advance, look for its website and do your research there. Although you won't find out which chair to avoid in the staffroom, you will learn something of the ethos of the school, recent successes and projects. Any information you can gain is useful. You may also know the parents of children who attend the school, and can chat to them informally about it.

---

### SUPPLY TEACHING TIP 4

Let the school know where you specialize and what you are willing to do. For example, if the school has to find cover for a practical GCSE lesson such as PE or textiles, it is preferable to find someone who can advise meaningfully on the subjects to someone who will have to supervise copying notes from a book while the practical coursework deadlines loom closer.

---

## The supply teacher in the classroom

At its best, supply teaching is about delivering your best classroom practice, being the 'visiting expert' and providing a different perspective. At its worst, it is about surviving until the bell goes!

### Survival tips

Be your own best cheerleader. Don't wait for someone else to congratulate you on a great teaching day or on surviving a terrible one. If you feel you have really made a difference today, taught well and even added that extra something, praise yourself. If you feel like crawling into a hole after a day of riots and lost cover work, still praise yourself. Be prepared to encounter both scenarios, and keep reminding yourself what a good job you are doing. Below are a few ways of dealing with the challenges you might face.

### Challenge: students pushing the boundaries

Some students are looking for a chink in the supply teacher's armour. Show that you know the school and are considered part of the staff, by using other teachers' names, and your knowledge of the school's systems, sanctions and rewards to show that you're to be taken seriously.

Think beforehand about how *you* run *your* classroom – what is allowed and what's unacceptable – in case you run into 'Mr So-and-So always lets us . . .' territory. Waver, and students will see your uncertainty. Be confident – 'Well, *I* expect . . .' – and most of the time they will accept your lead. It's good to provide continuity, but not at the expense of you losing authority in the classroom. You don't need to judge the regular teacher and set yourself against him (see all the students flock to defend!), just say that you do some things differently.

*Challenge: the cover work has been left elsewhere; the Head of Department 'will be along in a minute' to set work; the cupboards are locked; the books are in another classroom*

If you have a little time to fill in at the beginning of a lesson, using the Literacy and Numeracy Strategies' ideas of a 'starter activity' can be a lifesaver. Set a short puzzle or game while you send a student to find help.

For example:

- In an MFL lesson, students list in French objects they can see in the room – offer merits (or equivalent) for the longest/ most accurate/ most inventive lists.
- In a Science lesson, students create an alphabetical vocabulary list of scientific terms: acid, bunsen burner, carbonate, etc.
- In Design Technology, students have ten minutes to design a machine that delivers the cover work from the staffroom to the supply teacher at the desk, using pulleys and cog systems.

Using 'listing activities' has great value: they are easy to concentrate on, they can be finite and give a definite goal, and students will generally settle to them quickly.

*Challenge: no work has been set*

As a supply teacher, always have single, self-contained lessons either in your bag or in your head. Then if there is no work set, you can do something you want to do, and still make it a meaningful learning experience for the students. Try to tailor your lesson to the subject – you will become more skilled at this – but if you really can't, just don't worry about it and do your thing. In primary school, this is a great opportunity to have a full-day activity planned, such as an investigation or project that brings in skills from many different curriculum areas. Obviously, if you are covering a long-term absence, you need to stick to the literacy-numeracy timetables and so on, but a one-off day-long project can bring a welcome breath of fresh air to the primary classroom. Here are a few lesson ideas to get your own started:

- A class discussion: tell students which side they are to argue, give time to prepare in small groups, conduct a short class discussion, have students write a paragraph at the end arguing their case. Subjects can range from views on school uniforms to proving that Father Christmas does (or does not) exist. Oral skills are useful in any subject.
- The draw-your-own-shoe standby: minimal materials needed! Once students have got over the hurdle of 'I'm not sitting with Steven; his shoe stinks!' as well as students drawing (accurately and observantly) their shoes, you can make a subject focus: in Science, students concentrate on the materials and processes involved in the shoe; in English students consider and write about a day in the life of a shoe; in PE they design the best style of shoe for their favourite sporting activity.
- Take a class survey on any topic: favourite animals, where students shop, planned careers. Use the data in any number of ways: students draw charts, tables and graphs; plan a town high street for the age group's needs and wants; design the jacket of the book they have written when they have achieved their dreams.
- Ask students to write on a slip of paper the job they *hope* they will be doing in twenty years' time, and the job they think they will *really* be doing. Collect in the slips, then read aloud and see if students can guess whose is whose (this can also help you to learn names). This activity can extend in any number of ways.

### Challenge: joining in the staffroom
Notoriously difficult to become a part of, at its worst the staffroom can be simply an obstacle course of cliques and reserved chairs that the supply teacher has to negotiate. At its best it is a support network where you can find out everything you need to know (for example,

the fact that 8C is a nightmare for everyone, not just you). Mostly you will have to apologize your way into conversations or seats ('Sorry – I don't know where I can sit – is this okay?' 'Sorry – I don't know anyone, hi, I'm X . . .'). A staffroom full of people who all know each other can be daunting – smile and fake confidence if you don't feel it.

If the staffroom seems too daunting at lunchtimes, or you really are being ignored despite your best attempts, become involved in lunchtime activities instead. There might be an orchestra that needs some cymbals bashing, or a computer club that needs an extra technical brain on hand. If you've found a school that you like, it's a good way to get to know students (and for them to get to know you, beginning to eliminate the usual supply teacher discipline issues), and you'll get to know the member of staff too, giving you an 'in' in the staffroom.

*Challenge: an hour of repetitive work; students become restless after twenty minutes*
Most teachers try to set cover work that will involve minimal input from the supply teacher, partly because they don't want to put a non-specialist in an awkward position. Even so, it is worth trying to 'teach' at least a bit – start off with five or ten minutes asking the students questions about the topic, or a quick-fire mental activity. If you're faced with an hour of 'Answer questions 1 to 50 in sentences in your books', stop the students at intervals to discuss their responses. Find ways to bring the class back to a focus to keep opportunities for restless behaviour to a minimum.

## Making sure you're asked to come back

If you like the school and want to return, make sure you're the first name they think of when they reach for the phone for supply cover. Always leave notes for the absent teacher on each lesson you have taught. If the students didn't complete the work, note the point they reached in the lesson plan. Try to name a few students in praise for particularly good behaviour or work or for being helpful – it shows that you are on the ball and interested.

Note any behaviour issues, with names if you can. Again, it shows that you are keen to help the regular teacher by maintaining standards and continuity. It will also help you out when you return, as the regular teacher is able to follow up on your comments – showing the students that you are communicating and their behaviour, good or otherwise, will be acted upon.

At the end of your first day, and perhaps the next few, check in with someone – the teacher in charge of organizing cover or the head of the department, for example. Just let them know that you've survived and are still smiling and standing upright. Make them aware that you're keen to come back – and have your diary with you just in case.

When the supply teaching work begins to dry up in the summer months (even a slightly ill teacher can face school once Year 11 are on exam leave), you may look at . . .

## Becoming an assistant examiner

Many full-time teachers take on examining work during the summer. If you are in the first years of your career, there is still so much to do for your day job that marking as well may just be too much to handle. If you are a supply teacher, though, you are only limited by how long you can bear to sit in a chair, pen in hand!

## Is it for you?

Marking is a great way for supply teachers to keep up with the exam systems. It's professional development, updating and improving your skills. You set your own timetable, working at home under distant (usually telephoned) guidance from a team leader. Training meetings provide an opportunity to network with other education professionals. You have the privilege of reading the products of two years of hard work from the students. And . . . there's the cash.

You do need to be very disciplined. You will have to decide and stick to your quota of scripts per day based on the length of the examining period, and meet deadlines for samples of your marking within that time. You may have to reserve your own judgements in order to apply those dictated by the senior examiners. There is a *lot* of paperwork involved, checking and cross-checking, as you enter grades as numbers and letters and percentages. You need to be able to set aside your tiredness, your argument with your kids, your morning grumpies, to give all the candidates an equal and fair chance.

## The practicalities – jobs and pay

GCSE and SAT exam boards recruit all year round for examiners. It's usual to begin marking in the summer session of exams, and you should start thinking about applying in January at the latest. The exam boards have websites with the details you will need to contact them for application forms. Some even post their form on the website – you simply print it, fill it in and send it off. You will not normally be required to interview, but will be sent confirmation of your 'self-employment' as an examiner, details of training meetings, and a rough idea of your allocation of scripts.

### Finding out about the boards

A number of factors apply, though many simply amount to personal preference. The exam periods for different boards vary only slightly – expect to set aside any time from the end of May to the end of July. You may want to mark for a board whose syllabus you have taught, though you may find *not* having taught a particular board an advantage, as you will have no preconceived notions of the grading. You may have a preference for higher tier or foundation tier papers (or there may be no choice) – there will be very slight differences in the amount you are paid per paper.

### Training for examinership

As a new examiner, you will attend not only a standardization meeting but a new examiners' meeting prior to that: a sort of introduction to the board, the system and timetable, and probably a few past papers to give you an idea of what to expect at the standardization meeting.

A day or two after the students sit the exams, you will attend a standardization meeting. In teams, you work on sample scripts to get everyone using the criteria and beginning to mark in line with what the senior examiners have agreed. Then you will likely move onto some 'live' scripts, from the recent exam, and go through the same procedure. The standardization meeting will also help you to get used to using the correct notation on scripts – different for every exam board (some use code letters, some use numbers, some want comments written, others don't).

### The examining period

After standardization, you will have to submit an initial sample to your team leader, who will give you a few pointers on fine-tuning your marking and tell you to continue. In some cases you will be asked to send another sample, acting upon their advice. Some boards ask for samples when you're halfway through your allocation and again near the end. Don't panic – it's just to ensure things are still going along consistently, and to discover early on if you are having any difficulties so they can help you right away.

### Pay me – THANK YOU!

Payment for examining is generally more straightforward than for supply teaching: there is a set amount per script and a set allocation. If you don't quite finish your allocation, you will be paid for those scripts that you have marked. You will also be paid expenses for attending examiners' meetings – some boards are more strict than others about keeping receipts, so just keep everything (including a copy of the claim form) until you have been paid. Some boards require you to pay the postage you use to send samples and correspondence, and then claim this at the end of the exam period, while others send you prepaid stationery. Keep a record of phone calls to your team leader as you can claim for the cost of these too.

---

**ASSISTANT EXAMINER TIP 1**

Be wrong, and be bold! At the beginning, everyone tends to have wildly different ideas of how to grade a paper. You will gradually come into line with each other, and learning is easier if you are willing to give your ideas. The team leader will start to see your marking tendencies (very generous, slightly mean) and then can help you move towards standardization more easily.

BUT

Don't argue your case! You're there to bring your marking in line with what has been decided by the board, not to discuss what should be decided. You may just have to put aside what you think and accept what you are told. Arguing for an extra mark or a higher grade is pointless and it wastes everybody's time.

## Survival tips

### *If difficulties arise, don't panic*
Illnesses and other unforeseen circumstances can affect your ability to complete your allocation of marking. Exam boards are usually very understanding . . . *provided you tell them*. If for any reason you feel you aren't going to complete your allocation, contact your team leader at once so that your scripts can be sent to another examiner. Most boards will give you an extension of a few days or a week if you just feel you need a bit more time. Much better to tell them in advance than wait till the last minute and return unmarked scripts. It is highly unlikely that, if your marking is generally good, the exam board will think any less of you for not completing. People are human; life happens – and sometimes these things get in the way of marking exams.

### *Pace yourself*
Decide how many scripts you can realistically do in a day, and try to stick to it. As you get into the swing of marking, it will become quicker. The first ten or twenty are absolutely tortuous and you will convince yourself that you're never going to manage 400 in the next three weeks. You will agonize over single marks – a high C or a middle C??? – and feel that you will never learn the correct notation. IT GETS BETTER. After the first hundred you will probably be sailing along.

### *Realise your limits*
We all know the feeling – you stare at the page, it goes out of focus – what did they write in the last paragraph? Which question is this again? These criteria suddenly seem to be written in Hungarian! Is this an A or a D grade? STOP. You do neither yourself nor the candidate justice by trying to mark at this point. You will know when it has come. For some people, it's every thirty or so papers. For others, it's every two hours. When you get to it, recognize it, and just go and do something else.

### *Live by the treat*
You need treats to get through marking. Even when you have the most interesting exam paper in the world, with the liveliest and most

captivating responses, there comes a point where it is repetitive and (whisper it softly) rather boring and you need to keep yourself going. Maybe every twenty papers you have a biscuit (potentially dangerous for the diet as you get faster at marking). Maybe after three hours you take a walk along the river. Maybe when you have mailed your sample papers to the team leader, you call a friend for a chat. Treats get you through the boring parts of marking.

*Set your own timetable, and ignore others' advice*
You know how best you work. Some people can leap out of bed and mark twenty papers before seven a.m., others don't get started till nine at night and then work through till the early hours. Some mark steadily, with regular breaks: ten papers in the morning, ten in the afternoon, ten in the evening, while others pull a marking marathon, sitting down in the morning and not looking up from the desk until midnight. Don't be fazed if your team leader uses one method and you another – so long as you get to the same place in the end, it doesn't matter.

---

### SUPPLY TEACHER/ASSISTANT EXAMINER CONCLUDING TIPS

- Keep on top of paperwork. As you are now in a sense your own boss, keep everything, especially if it's related to your pay!
- Continue to cultivate your professional relationships. Extend your contacts through new schools and through networking at examiners' meetings.
- If you have decided to make these changes in your career, make them with confidence. See them as an opportunity to extend your skills and open new doors in directions you hadn't considered before.

---

*Part Six*

# Endings?

# 13 Epilogue

*Angela Thody*

## Smile – you're on stage now

This book opened with the teacher's image – dress to impress your audience. This sounds as if you're an actor rather than a teacher – but reflect on how applicable is that analogy.

Actors need to look as if they own the stage (the classroom) and to project their voices so that they command attention. The audience 'watching' you will be pupils, parents, the governors and the wider school community.

The cast sharing the stage with you are your colleagues who teach with you. Support staff will have duplicated the play for you and organized some of the props, the catering, the cleaning and 'front-of-house' activities such as the box office where the pupils enrol.

In the prompt corner, managing the production budget and auditing the accounts, being responsible for health and safety legalities, you'll find the school bursar and administrators.

Producing and financing the play are those whose job is to keep schools in line with what is wanted by the politicians. In England, these include, amongst others, the Secretary of State for Education, the Department for Education and Skills, the Office for Standards in Education, the Teacher Training Agency (TTA) and the local education authorities.

This is a post-modern play so there is only an outline script for you (the National Curriculum and external examination syllabuses), but the play is directed by your subject co-ordinators, heads of departments, year tutors, deputy headteachers and headteachers, professional development staff, mentors and advanced skills teachers.

Meanwhile, you still have the enjoyment of writing most of your own script and choosing your costumes and props. Your interpretations as an actor will largely determine the success of the play.

Like any actor, no doubt you will have stage fright sometimes. That's the moment to do two things:

First, take a lesson from commerce. When Disneyland's employees leave their changing room, they are told they are thenceforth on stage, whether they are Donald Duck in a costume or the person who cleans up after the horses in the parade. Everyone helps to create the image – smile, look happy – it's contagious.

You'll notice this on parents' evenings. The teachers will usually change into something different from the clothes they have been wearing during the day. It's an acknowledgement that the audience has changed and, therefore, the image too needs changing.

Secondly, remember you're a consummate actor. When you enter the classroom feeling slightly less than assured, regard yourself as an actor. The audience won't know the script as well as you do and if you look, and sound, as if you know what you are doing, they will think that you're confident.

You'll find, as do all teachers at some point, that you have under-estimated the amount of material you need to fill the lesson, or that the teacher in charge of personal and social education was away ill and so you didn't get the notes for tutor time this week, or you've exhausted the reception class views on their family and holidays.

With the tips from this book, you'll feel confident enough to fill the time by leading a discussion on what your pupils think makes a successful teacher. Have a lead-in sentence or two prepared for this (standard assertiveness technique). Then, when you've heard your pupils' views, check them out in comparison with those we've suggested in this book.

Meanwhile, read on . . .

the most off-putting thing about starting teaching has been the reactions of other teachers on hearing my choice of profession! It seems that people already in the job want to do their best to stop unsuspecting graduates from joining the ranks. Obviously . . . we have to go in prepared for a lot of setbacks and some demoralizing times, but if there weren't any good bits people wouldn't be teachers at all. (Teacher in training for secondary school teaching, 1999)

There are many 'good bits'. If you're new to teaching, enjoy the dis-covery of them. If you're more experienced, enjoy inducting others into those good bits. And let successful teaching generate ever more good bits.

# Bibliography

**Part One: Beginnings**

Bleach, K. (1999) *The Induction and Mentoring of Newly Qualified Teachers*. London: David Fulton.

Galton, M., Hargreaves, L., Comber, C., Wall, D. and Pell, T. (1999) 'Changes in patterns of teacher interaction in primary classrooms: 1976–1996', *British Educational Research Journal*, 25(1), 23–38.

Helsby, G. and McCulloch, G. (1996) 'Teacher professionalism and curriculum control', in I. Goodson and A. Hargreaves (eds) *Teachers' Professional Lives*. London: Falmer Press.

O'Sullivan, F., Thody, A. M. and Wood, E. (2000) *From Bursar to School Business Manager*. London: Financial Times Publishing.

Spark, M. (1969) *The Prime of Miss Jean Brodie*. London: Penguin.

Weber, S. and Mitchell, C. (1996) 'Using drawings to interrogate professional identity and the popular culture of teaching', in I. Goodson and A. Hargreaves (eds) *Teachers' Professional Lives*. London: Falmer Press.

**Part Two: Success with Pupils**

Bryson, J. (1998) *Effective Classroom Management*. London: Hodder and Stoughton.

Covey, S. R. (1989) *The Seven Habits of Highly Effective People*. London and New York: Simon and Schuster.

Craig, I. (1997) *Managing Primary Classrooms*. London: Pitman Publishing.

Fritzell, B. (1996) 'Voice disorders and occupations', *Logopedics Phoniatrics Vocology*, 21(1), 7–12.

Galton, M., Hargreaves, L., Comber, C., Wall, D. and Pell, T. (1999) 'Changes in patterns of teacher interaction in primary classrooms: 1976–1996', *British Educational Research Journal*, 25(1), 23–38.

Gotaas, C. and Starr, C. D. (1993) 'Vocal fatigue among teachers', *Folio Phoniatrica*, 45, 120–9.

Harris, T., Harris, S., Rubin, J. S. and Howard, D. M. (1998) *The Voice Clinic Handbook*. London: Whurr Publishers.

McPhillimy, B. (1996) *Controlling Your Class*. Chichester: Wiley and Son.

Morton, V. and Watson, D. R. (1998) 'The teaching voice: problems and perceptions', *Logopedics Phoniatrics Vocology*, 23(3), 133–9.

Mosley, J. (1996) *Quality Circle Time.* Cambridge: LDA.

O'Brien, T. (1998) *Promoting Positive Behaviour.* London: David Fulton.

Rogers, W. (1998) *You Know the Fair Rule.* London: Pitman Publishing.

Smith, E., Kirchner, H. L., Taylor, M., Hoffman, J. and Lemke, J. (1998) 'Voice problems among teachers: differences by gender and teaching characteristics', *Journal of Voice*, 24(3), 49–54.

Thurman, L. and Welch, G. (1997) *Bodymind and Voice: Foundations of Voice Education.* Iowa City, Iowa: National Centre for Voice and Speech.

Titze, I. R. (1994) *Principles of Voice Production.* Englewood Cliffs, NJ: Prentice Hall.

Vygotsky, L. S. (1978) *Mind in Society.* Cambridge, MA: Harvard University Press.

**Part Three: Success with Colleagues**

Bush, T. and Middlewood, D. (eds) (1997) *Managing People in Education.* London: Paul Chapman Publishing.

Everard, K. and Morris, G. (3rd edn) (1996) *Effective School Management.* London: Paul Chapman Publishers.

Gann, N. (1998) *Improving School Governance: How Better Governors Make Better Schools.* London: Falmer Press.

O'Sullivan, F., Thody, A. M. and Wood, E. (2000) *From Bursar to School Business Manager.* London: Financial Times Publishing.

Partington, J., Stacey, B. and Turland, A. (1998) *Governing Independent Schools.* London: David Fulton.

Thody, A. M. (1994) *School Governors: Leaders or Followers?* Harlow: Longman.

**Part Four: Success with Yourself**

Cains, R. A. and Brown, C. R. (1998a) 'Newly qualified teachers: a comparative analysis of perceptions held by B.Ed. and PGCE trained primary teachers of the level and frequency of stress experienced during the first year of teaching', *Educational Psychology*, 18(1), 97–110.

Caplan, G. (1964) *Principles of Preventive Psychiatry.* New York: Basic Books.

Carrington, P. (1999) *The Power of Letting Go: a Practical Approach to Relaxing the Pressure of Your Life.* Shaftesbury: Element.

Cooper, C. L. and Straw, A. (2nd edn) (1998) *Successful Stress Management In A Week.* London: Headway.

Covey, S. R., Merrill, A. R. and Merrill, R. R. (1997) *First Things First Every Day Because Where You're Headed Is More Important Than How Fast You're Going.* London and New York: Simon and Schuster.

Dunham, J. (2nd edn) (1992) *Stress in Teaching.* London: Routledge.

Newton, T., Handy, J. and Fineman, S. (1995) *Managing Stress: Emotion and Power at Work.* London: Sage.

Pollock, K. (1988) 'On the nature of social stress: production of a modern mythology', *Social Science and Medicine*, 26, 381–92.

Wilson, P. (1998) *Calm at Work.* London: Penguin.

Woodcock, M. (1982) *The Unblocked Manager.* Aldershot: Gower.

### Part Five: Success with Your Career

Cains, R. A. and Brown, C. R. (1998b) 'Newly qualified teachers: a comparison of perceptions held by primary and secondary teachers of their training routes and of their early experiences in post', *Educational Psychology,* 18(3), 341–52.

Goodson, I. and Hargreaves, A., (eds) *Teachers' Professional Lives.* London: Falmer Press.

Hicks, D. and Slaughter, R. (eds) (1998) *Futures Education: World Yearbook of Education.* London: Kogan Page.

Hilsum, S. and Start, K. B. (1974) *Promotion and Careers in Teaching.* Slough: NFER Publishing.

Hodgkinson, P. (1998) 'The origins of a theory of career decision-making: a case study of hermeneutical research', *British Educational Research Journal,* 24(5), 557–72.

Hutchinson, F. (1996) *Educating Beyond Violent Futures.* London: Routledge.

Maclean, R. (1992) *Teachers; Careers and Promotion Patterns.* London: Falmer Press.

Moos, L., Mahony, P. and Reeves, J. (1998) 'What teachers, parents, governors and pupils want from their heads', in Macbeth, J. (ed.) *Effective School Leadership: Responding to Change.* London: Paul Chapman Publishing.

Peters, T. J. (1995) *The Pursuit of Wow! Every Person's Guide to Topsy-Turvey Times.* London: Macmillan.

Thody, A. M. (1993) *Developing Your Career in Education Management.* Harlow: Longman.

Whitacker, P. (1997) *Primary Schools and the Future: Celebration, Challenges and Choices.* Buckingham: Open University Press.

# Useful addresses

## Part One: Beginnings

Centre for the Study of Comprehensive Schools
University of Leicester, Moulton College, Moulton, Northampton
NN3 7RR
01604 492337; www.cscs.org.uk; lizacs@rmplc.co.uk

College of Teachers
Coppice Row, Epping, Essex, CM16 7DN
01992 812727; collegeofteachers@mailbox.ulcc.ac.uk

Department for Education and Skills
Sanctuary Buildings, Great Smith Street, London SW1P 3BT
0870 000 2288; 0870 001 2345 (general enquiries);
0845 60 22260 (publications); www.dfes.gov.uk

General Teaching Council England
3rd Floor, Cannon House, 24 The Priory Queensway, Birmingham
B4 6BS
346-354 Grays Inn Road, Lndon WCCX 8BP
0870 001 0308; www.gtce.org.uk

General Teaching Council Scotland
Clerwood House, 96 Clemiston Road, Edinburgh EH12 6UT
0131 314 6000; gtcs@gtcs.org.uk

National Assembly for Wales – Training and Education Department
Crown Buildings, Cathays Park, Cardiff, CF10 3NQ
029 2082 5111

National Association for Primary Education
University of Leicester, Moulton College, Moulton, Northampton
NN3 7RR
01604 647669; www.nape.org.uk; nationaloffice@nape.org.uk

Northern Ireland Council for the Curriculum, Examinations and Assessment
Clarendon Dock, 29 Clarendon Road, Belfast, BT1 3BG
028 9026 1200; www.ccea.org.uk; info@ccea.org.uk

Northern Ireland Department of Education
Rathgael House, Balloo Road, Bangor, County Down, BT19 7PR
028 9127 9279; mail@deni-gov.uk; www.deni.gov.uk

Office for Standards in Education
Alexandra House, 33 Kingsway, London WC2B 6 SE
020 7421 6800; www.ofsted.gov.uk

Qualifications and Curriculum Authority
83 Piccadilly, London W1J 8QA
020 7509 5555; www.qca.org.uk; info@qca.org.uk

Scottish Executive Education Deparment
Victoria Quay, Edinburgh, EH6 6QQ
0131 556 8400/0845 774 1741

Teacher Training Agency
Portland House, Stag Place, London SW1E 5TF
020 7925 3700

Teacher Training Agency Communications Centre
P O Box 3210, Chelmsford, Essex, CM1 3WA
01245 454454; teaching@ttainfo.demon.co.uk

Welsh Secondary Schools' Association
Gwalia House, 124 Walter Road, Swansea SA1 5RF
01792 455933

## Part Two: Success with Pupils

Association for Language Teaching
150 Railway Terrace, Rugby, Warks, CV21 3HN
01788 546443; langlearn@all-languages.org.uk; www.all-languages.org.uk

Association of Teachers of Mathematics
7 Shaftesbury Street, Derby DE23 8YB
01332 346599

Association of Workers for Children with Emotional and Behavioural
Difficulties
Charlton Court, East Sutton, Maindstone, Kent ME17 3DQ
01622 843104; www.awce.co.uk; awce@mistral.co.uk

Basic Skills Agency
7th Floor, Commonwealth House, 1–19 New Oxford Street,
London WC1A 1NU
020 7405 4017; www.basic-skills.co.uk; enquiries@basic-skills.co.uk

British Association for Early Childhood Education
136 Cavell Street, London, E1 2JA
020 7539 5400; office@early-education.org.uk

British Association of Teachers of the Deaf
21 The Haystacks, High Wycombe, Bucks., HP13 6PY
01494 464190; www.batod.org.uk

British Dyslexia Association
98 London Road, Reading RG1 5AU
0118 935 1927; www.bda-dyslexia.org.uk; info@dyslexiahelp-bda-demon.co.uk

British Institute of Learning Disabilities
Wolverhampton Road, Kidderminster DY10 3PP
01562 850251; bild@bild.demon.co.uk

Centre for Information on Language Teaching and Research
20 Bedfordbury, Covent Garden, London WC2N 4LB
020 7379 5101; confs.direct@cilt.org.uk; www.cilt.org.uk

Centre for Studies on Inclusive Education
Newredland, Frenchhay Campus, Coldharbour Lane, Bristol BS16 1QU
0117 344 4007; www.inclusion.org.uk

Commonwealth Institute
Kensington High Street, London W8 6NQ
020 7603 4535; www.commonwealth.org.uk;
info@commonwealth.org.uk

Design and Technology Association
16 Wellesbourne House, Walton Road, Wellesbourne, Warks. CV35 9JB
01789 470007; data@data.org.uk

Economics and Business Education Association
1a Keymer Road, Hassocks, West Sussex, BN6 8AD
01273 846033; ebeah@pavilion.co.uk

The English Association
University of Leicester, School of Education, University Road,
Leicester LE1 7RB
0116 252 3982

The Geographical Association
  160 Solly Street, Sheffield S1 4BF
  0114 296 0088; www.geography.org.uk

Joint Association of Classical Teachers
  Senate House, Malet Street, London WC1E 7HU
  020 7862 8706; www.jact.org.uk; jact@sas.org.uk

National Association for Gifted Children
  Suite 14, Challenge House, Sherwood Drive, Bletchley, Milton Keynes,
  MK3 6DP
  0870 770 3217; nagc@britain.org.uk

National Association of Music Educators
  Gordon Lodge, Snitterton Road, Matlock, Derbys. DE4 3L7
  www.name.org.uk

National Association for Pastoral Care in Education
  Institute of Education, University of Warwick, Coventry CV4 7AL
  024 7652 3810; www.napc@warwick.ac.uk; base@napce.org.uk

National Association for Special Educational Needs
  Nasan House, 4/5 Amber Business Village, Amber Close, Amington,
  Tamworth B77 4RP
  www.nasen.org.uk; welcome@nasen.org.uk

National Association for the Teaching of English
  50 Broadfield Road, Broadfield Business Centre, Sheffield S8 0XJ
  0114 255 5419; www.natehq@btconnect.com

National Council for School Sport
  95 Boxley Drive, West Bridgford, Nottingham NG2 7GN
  0115 923 1229; schoolsport@ntlworld.com

National Society for Promoting Religious Education
  Church House, Great Smith Street, London SW1P 3NZ
  020 7898 1491; info@natsoc.c-of-e.org.uk

Physical Education Association of the United Kingdom
  Building L25, London Road, Reading RG1 5AG
  www. pea.uk.com; enquiries@pea.uk.com

## Part Three: Success with Colleagues

*Bursars*
Independent Schools Bursars' Association
Unit 11–12, Manor Farm, Cliddesden, Basingstoke, Hants. RG25 2JB
01256 330369; isbasing@compuserve.com

MBA for School Bursars
IIEL, University of Lincoln, Brayford Pool, Lincoln LN1 7RF
01522 886169; iiel@lincoln.ac.uk

National Bursars Association
PO Box 12, Chard, Somerset TA20 3YX
01460 65628; www.nba.org.uk; RickardPV@aol.com

*Faith schooling*
Agency for Jewish Education
Bet Meir, 44a Albert Road, London NW4 2SJ
020 8457 9700

Catholic Federation of Teachers
24 Knowlands, Monkspath, Solihull, West Midlands, B90 4UG
0121 745 4265

Church of England Board of Education
Church House, Great Smith Street, London, SW1P 3NZ
020 7898 1500

Muslim Teachers' Association
146 Park Road, London NW8 7RG
020 7724 3363/4

*Governors*
National Association of Governors and Managers
Suite 1, 4th Floor, Western House, Small Brock. Queensway, Birmingham
B5 4HQ
0121 643 5787; www.nagm.org.uk; governorhq@nagm.org.uk

National Governors' Council
Glebe House, Church Street, Crediton, Devon EX17 2AF
01363 774377; ngc@ngc.org.uk

*Lobby groups for education*
Campaign for State Education
158 Durham Road, London SW20 0DG
020 8944 8206; www.casenet.org.uk; case@casenet.org.uk

### Parents

National Confederation of Parent Teacher Associations
    18 St Johns Hill, Sevenoaks, Kent, TN13 3NA
    01732 748850; www.ncpt.org.uk; info@ncpta.org.uk

Parent Teacher Association of Wales
    5 St Bridges Close, Llanyrafon, Cwmbran NP44 8SL
    01623 34067

### Teachers' professional associations and unions

Association of Secondary Teachers, Ireland
    ASTI House, Winterhavern Street, Dublin 8
    info@asti_ie

Association of Teachers and Lecturers
    2 Northumberland Street, London, WC2N 5RD
    020 2930 6441; www.askatl.org.uk

Association of Teachers and Lecturers Northern Ireland
    397a Holywood Road, Belfast BT4 2LY
    028 9047 1412

Association of Teachers and Lecturers Wales
    First Floor, Empire House, Mount Stuart Square, Cardiff CF10 5FN
    029 2046 5000

Irish National Teachers' Organization
    35 Parnell Square, Dublin 1 and 23 College Gardens, Belfast BT9 6BS
    00 3531 8722533/028 9038 1455; info@info.ie

National Association of Schoolmasters/Union of Women Teachers
    Hillscourt Education Centre, Rednal, Birmingham B45 8RS
    0121 453 6150; www.teachersunion.org.uk; nasuwt@mail.nasuwt.org.uk

National Association of Schoolmasters/Union of Women Teachers (Scotland)
    34 West George Street, Glasgow, G2 1DA
    0141 332 0608

National Association of the Teachers of Wales
    Prif Swyddfa, UCAC, Pen Roc, Rhodfa'r Mor, Aberystwyth SY23 2AZ
    01970 615577

National Union of Teachers
    Hamilton House, Mabledon Place, London WC1H 9BD
    020 7388 6191

The Professional Association of Teachers
  2 St James Court, Friar Gate, Derby DE1 1BT
  01332 372337; hq@pat.org.uk; www.pat.org.uk

The Professional Association of Teachers in Scotland
  4/6 Oak Lane, Edinburgh EH12 6XH
  0131 317 8282; scotland@pat.org.uk

Scottish Secondary Teachers' Association
  15 Dundas Street, Edinburgh EH3 6QG
  0131 556 5919; www.ssta.org.uk; info@ssta.org.uk

Ulster Teachers' Union
  94 Malone Road, Belfast BT9 5HP
  028 906 62216

Welsh Teachers' Union – Undeb Cenedlaethal Athrawon Cymru
  Swyddfa UCAL, Pen Roc, Aberystwyth, Cereduyion, SY23 2A2
  ucac@athrawon.com; www.athrawon.com

## Part Four: Success with Yourself

British Association for Counselling and Psychotherapy
  1 Regent Place, Rugby, Warks CV21 2PJ
  0870 443 5252; www.bacp.co.uk; bacp@bacp.co.uk

TBF: the Teacher Support Network
  Hamilton House, Mabledon Place, London WC1H 9BE
  020 7544 5200; www.teachersupport.org.uk; tbf@teachersupport.org.uk

Teacherline – England
  A telephone counselling service, part funded by the DfES.
  0800 562 561 (any time)

Teacherline – Wales
  0800 085 5088 (any time)

Teachers' Pension Agency
  Mowden Hall, Staindrop Road, Darlington, DL3 9BG
  01325 460155

## Part Five: Success with Your Career

### *Alternative jobs*
Government departments – national, regional and local. Those concerned
with employment offer lists of job placements, training and advice,
counselling and placements.

**Business opportunities/experiences**
Business Link – this advises on setting up your own business
  0345 567765

Flying Pig – an example of a company set up by an ex-teacher, marketing
paper engineering
  www.flying-pig.co.uk

Hope Education, Orb Mill, Huddersfield Road, Oldham OL4 2ST.
  This company is interested in developing and marketing teachers' ideas for
  resources. They have an introductory pack.
  0161 628 2788/020 7628 5957

Teacher Placement Service
  Understanding British Industry c/o The Royal Mail, The Loft,
  9 Howick Place, London SW1P 1AA
  020 7592 8844

Banks – these usually have advice leaflets on setting up your own business and
how to make and present a business plan in order to secure loans.

**Career guidance**
Career Analysis Ltd, Career House, Mill Lane, Cambridge, CB2 1XE
enquiries@careers.cam.ac.uk; wwwcareers.cam.ac.uk;
www.careeranalysts.co.uk

Educational Guidance Survey for Adults
  4th Floor, Linenhall Street, Belfast BT2 8BA
  028 9024 4274; info@egsa.org.uk

**Consultancy, advice, inspection – offering nationwide opportunities**
Cambridge Educational Associates
  Demeter House, Station Road, Cambridge CB1 2RS
  01223 578500; cea@cea.org.uk; www.cea.org.uk

Council for British Teachers
  60 Queens Road, Reading RG1 4BS
  0118 902 1000; enquiries at cfbt.com

National Association of Education Inspectors, Advisers and Consultants
  Woolley Hall, Woolley, Wakefield, W. Yorks, WF4 2JR
  01226 383420; naeiac@gemsoft.org; www.naeiac.org

Society of Education Consultants
  25 Dickenson Road, London, N8 9ER
  sec@sec.org.uk; www.sec.org.uk

### Courses for career development
Local education authorities
> Ask your local one for a directory of adult and community education courses and for courses provided by local authorities for retraining into other careers. These are often funded by government agencies, such as the European Union, and target employment minorities, e.g. minority ethnic groups, long-term unemployed, women.

Local universities and colleges
> See your local telephone book for local courses.

John Wilson – runs short courses for teachers wanting to escape teaching.
> 01736 797061

Women In Management – helps you to network and runs training and development seminars.
> 020 7382 9978

Women Returners' Network – offer advice to women wanting to return to employment outside the home and publish *Returning to Work*, a directory of education and training for women.
> 100 Park Village East, London NW1 3SR
> 020 7839 8188

### Examining boards
Assessment and Qualifications Alliance(AQA)
> Stag Hill House, Guildford, Surrey GU2 7XJ
> 01483 506506; www.aqa.org.uk

City and Guilds
> 1 Giltspur Street, London Ec1E 9DD
> 020 72942800; www.city-and-guilds.co.uk

Edexcel
> Stewart House, 32 Russell Square, London WC1B 5DN
> 0870 240 8900; enquiries@edexcel.org.uk; www.edexcel.org.uk

English Speaking Board (International) Ltd
> 26a Princes Street, Southport, Merseyside PR8 1EQ
> 01704 501 730; admin@esbuk.demon.co.uk

Independent Schools Council information service (ISCis)
> Jordan House, Christchurch Road, New Milton, Hants. BH25 6QJ
> 01425 621111; ce@iseb.co.uk; www.isis.org.uk

International Baccalaureat Organisation Curriculum and Assessment Centre
 Peterson House, Fortran Road, St Mellors, Cardiff, CF3 0WB
 029 2077 4000; ibca@ibo.org.uk; www.ibo.org

Joint Council for General Qualifications
 Joint Examining Board, 30a Dyer Street, Cirencester, Glos GL7 2PF
 01285 641747; jeb@jeb.co.uk; www.jeb.co.uk

OCR (Oxford, Cambridge and RSA)
 1 Regent Street, Cambridge, CB2 1GG
 01223 552552; www.ocr.org.uk; helpdesk@ocr.org.uk

Scottish Qualifications Authority (SQA)
 Hanover House, 24 Douglas Street, Glasgow G2 7NQ
 0141 248 7900

Welsh Joint Education Committee
 245 Western Avenue, Cardiff CF5 2YX
 029 2026 5000; www.wjec.co.uk

*Franchising or other opportunities to help you set up as a tutor*
Jamtart Art Workshops, 65 Third Avenue, Teignmouth, Devon TQ14 9DP
 0845 1 304630

Kumon Maths and Reading – www.kumon.com/www.kumon.co.uk
Stagecoach (theatre arts) – www. stagecoach.co.uk

*Grants for re-training*
British Federation of Women Graduates – grants to complete degree studies
 4 Mandeville Courtyard, 142 Battersea Park Road, London SW11 4NB

*Independent schools*
Girls' Day School Trust
 100 Rochester Row, London SW1P 1JP
 020 7393 6666

Girls' Schools Association
 130 Regent Road, Leicester LE1 7PG
 0116 2541619; www.girls-schools.org.uk; office@girls.schools.org.uk

Independent Schools Council Information Service
 www.iscis.uk.net

*International opportunities*
The British Council
 10 Spring Gardens, London SW1A 2BN
 020 7930 8466

Central Bureau for Educational Visits and Exchanges
10 Spring Gardens, London SW1A 2BN
020 7389 4004

Council of International Schools
www.cois.org

Council of International Schools in the Americas
www.cista.org

European Council of International Schools (ECIS)
www.ecis.org

League for the Exchange of Commonwealth Teachers
Commonwealth House, 7 Lion Square, Tremadoc Road, London
SW4 7NQ
020 7498 1101

Service Children's Education
HQ SCE (UK), Trenchard Lines, Upavon, Pewsey, Wiltshire SN9 6BE
01980 618244; mod.sce.uk@gtnet.gov.uk

Voluntary Service Overseas
317 Putney Bridge Road, London SW15 2PN
020 8780 2266

Winston Churchill Memorial Trust – Travelling Fellowships
15 Queen's Gate Terrace, London SW7 5PR

### Leadership and management
National College for School Leadership
0870 001 1155; ncsl-office@ncsl.org.uk; www.ncsl.org.uk

Several universities have dedicated leadership centres offering degrees, diplomas and short courses, e.g.
Centre for Education Leadership and Management, University of Leicester
www.le.ac.uk/se/centres/celm
International Institute for Education Leadership, University of Lincoln
iiel@lincoln.ac.uk

### Supply teaching
Agencies – advertise weekly in the *Times Educational Supplement*

Local Education Authorities – consult the Yellow Pages for phone numbers

# Index

ABC teaching approach   27, 33
acoustics
    classroom   50
    voice   55
adult education   4, 78, 138, 151, 161
advanced skills teacher   15, 138, 181
ageism   155
agency teaching *see* substitute teaching
anger   44, 71, 86
ancillaries *see* support staff
anticipation   121–4, 130–4
anxiety   121–4, 128, 130–4
appraisal   ix, 8, 74, 100, 145
assertiveness   69, 70–2, 108, 182
Australia   14, 142

behaviour (pupils) *see* pupils
behaviour management *see* classroom management, pupil management
behaviour policy *see* rules
bursars   98, 159

career   ix, 14–15, Part Four *passim,* 193
career resume *see* c.v.
circle time   22–3, 45–6
classroom agreements   23, 37
classroom assistants   97, 98, 131, 133; *see also* support staff
classroom management   19–38, 61, 97, 131, 164, 169, 170–3
colleagues   8–11, 65–74, 75–90, 108, 110, 117, 119, 131, 132, 133, 149, 172, 181, 190
Commonwealth   138, 188
communication
    with pupils   23, 24
    with colleagues   67, 74, 81, 83–6, 96, 110, 141
conflict with colleagues   86–90
    with parents   87–8
    with pupils   *see* pupils' behaviour management
consultancy   145, 160, 193
cover teaching *see* agency teaching
c.v. (curriculum vitae)   149–52, 157, 166

delight   121–4, 130–4
defiance   43
delegation   116–17
demotivation   65–7
DfES (Department for Education and Skills)   15, 110, 158, 181, 186
difficult pupils *see* pupils' behaviour management
distress   121–4, 128, 130–4

(EAZ) Education Action Zone   158
emotional awareness (teachers')   67, 76–7, 132
equal opportunities   6, 144
ERO (Education Review Office, New Zealand)   9
Europe   138
examinations   97, 144, 152, 158; *see also* marking

faith schools   99, 147, 190
filing   110–11
further education *see* adult education

GCSE (General Certificate in Secondary Education)   163, 175
governors   3, 11–13, 74, 91, 99–101, 138, 143, 152, 158, 181, 190

headteacher   10, 15, 74, 78, 79, 89, 99, 100, 101, 117, 124
    career as   137, 141, 142, 143, 144, 146

image (teachers)   4, 16, 157, 181, 182
independent schools   96, 99, 138, 140, 142, 147, 195

larynx   50, 51, 52, 53, 55,
league tables   132, 143,
learning environment   19–38,
learning and teaching   32–6
leadership *see* headteacher and senior management
leisure   13–14, 105, 107, 128, 138
lesson preparation   5–6, 123, 124, 126
lifelong education *see* adult education

local education authorities (LEAs – UK)  12, 98, 99, 110, 138, 142, 147, 159, 166, 167, 181

management training  146
managing difficult situations  39
marking, 5, 6–8, 111–12, 131, 138, 151, 163, 174–8, 194–5
meetings  66, 93, 94, 101, 112–16, 132, 152
mentor  15, 20, 74, 97, 146, 149, 151, 158, 181
middle management  138
motivation  65–7, 68, 74, 76–80, 141, 156

National College for School Leadership  15, 146, 159, 196
National Curriculum  15, 98, 100, 121, 133, 181
national work time agreement  2003, 13, 103
negotiation  23, 71, 87, 88
New Zealand  9, 99
noise  31, 44
non-teaching staff *see* support staff
NQT (Newly Qualified Teacher)  9, 167

OFSTED (Office for Standards in Education)  8, 82, 100, 181, 186

parents  3, 11–13, 74, 40, 87, 89, 91–5, 97, 99, 100, 120, 133, 152, 181, 191
part-time teaching  151, 161
pastoral  80, 142, 150
PPA time (planning, preparation and assessment)  13
praise  29, 35–6, 41, 131, 170
primary schools  171, 172, 186
   careers in  137, 141, 150, 158
   parents' meetings in  93, 94
   meetings in  115
   stress in  120
   support staff in  96
   teams in  80
preventative behaviour strategies  36–8, 42
principal *see* headteacher
professional associations for teachers *see* unions
professional development *see* staff development
pupils
   achievements  14, 93
   behaviour and learning  15, 20–1, 23, 25–7, 32–6, 39–46, 61, 69, 91, 122, 169
   conflicts with  9–46, 88–9, 127, 169
   management of  3–8, 14, 19–38, 88, 89, 100
   records  9, 43, 97
   responsibilities  19–21
   rights  19–21
   and teachers' careers  139, 135
   and teachers' images  3–4, 181

and teacher stress  121, 122, 127, 128
self-esteem  6, 22, 24, 39
violence  42

qualifications  138, 145–7, 150, 187

redundancy  100, 161, 162
relief teaching *see* agency teaching
reports  11, 83, 93, 94, 95, 97, 100, 108, 131
rules, 22–3, 39–41, 168

SATS (Standard Attainment Tests)  163, 175
school boards/districts (USA) *see* local education authorities
School Teachers Pay and Conditions 2003 *see* national work time agreement
secondary schools
   careers in  137, 141, 142, 150
   marking  6–8, 131
   parents' meetings in  93, 94
   teachers' images  4
   teams in  80
self-esteem (teachers')  66, 68, 69, 70–2, 74
self-evaluation  28, 81
senior management  3, 10, 15, 79, 80, 82, 90, 99, 159, 96, 107, 110, 115, 116, 117, 124, 129, 138, 141
shouting  44
special measures  143
special needs  100, 138, 158, 189
special schools  96, 141, 143, 147, 167
staff development  ix, 74, 100, 137, 138, 145–7, 151, 174, 194
stress  41, 60, 105, 110, 119–29
stress management  13, 130–4
students *see* pupils
substitute teaching *see* supply teaching
support staff  3, 9, 10, 11–13, 14, 20, 61, 71, 73, 78, 91, 93, 95–8, 158, 133, 181, 190
supply teaching  146, 159, 164–74, 196
swearing  42

teams  9, 80–83, 106, 107, 156
teachers' assistants *see* support staff
time management  13, 81, 93, 94, 105–18,
TTA (Teacher Training Agency)  181, 187

unions  12, 13, 137, 138, 147, 151, 152, 191–2
USA  14, 48, 49, 120, 155
university  137, 145, 146, 147, 158, 161, 196

violent behaviour  42
vocal folds  51, 52, 53, 54, 55, 56, 61
vocal tract  42, 55, 56, 57, 58, 61
voice resonance  60

working hours  13, 103, 105, 126, 128–9